CONFUSION
INCORPORATED
A COLLECTION OF LIES, HOAXES & HIDDEN TRUTHS

BY STEWART HOME

CODEX

Confusion Incorporated:
A Collection Of Lies, Hoaxes & Hidden Truths
by Stewart Home

Published in 1999 by
Codex Books, PO Box 148, Hove, BN3 3DQ, UK

ISBN 1 899598 11 1

Printed by Caledonian International Book
Manufacturing Ltd, Glasgow, Scotland

CONTENTS

INTRODUCTION

MOST OF WHAT FOLLOWS was written under the threat of eviction, court action over debts or detention in mental institutions. Nearly all my journalism has been produced under the pressures of tight deadlines and out of desperation for money. However, the fact that my work is often error-ridden and misleading cannot be put down to drink. Indeed, what bourgeois sensibilities perceive as the faults in my prose are actually the direct result of an overweening desire to make the world a better place. While I have on occasion been forced to write about the piss-poor state of contemporary culture, I would much rather invent an art movement that for a few moments makes this planet seem like a funkier and more interesting place. Sure, the authority figures taken in by my japes tend to get mad if they realise their 'social inferiors' are laughing at them, but then hoaxes have long acted as the glue binding together the vast range of discourses I've assembled under the rubric of proletarian post-modernism.

Notoriously the broadsheet journalist Charlotte O'Sullivan read my spoof Glop Art feature in *The Big Issue* (27/5/96) and produced an article on this non-existent 'movement' for *The Observer* (30/6/96) without ever realising that the piece she'd ripped off was a hoax! Okay, so it wasn't quite as straight-forward as this. O'Sullivan wanted to plagiarise my article but was afraid she was being had. She phoned me and asked if I could put her in touch with any Glop artists. I said this might be difficult since, despite the obvious aesthetic merits of modifying posters in subway stations by obliterating parts of them with chewing gum, technically this practice constituted littering and was thus illegal. As a result Glop artists were reluctant to talk to journalists about their work, since they were all paranoid about getting busted by the transport police. As soon as O'Sullivan hung up I got one of my mates to call her back and pretend that he was a Glop artist. This was more than enough to convince a lazy journalist that my story was genuine.

Having devoted a paragraph of this introduction to the article 'Chew On This' from *The Big Issue,* some readers may wonder why I've not included it in the present collection. The answer to this is simple, you can find it on pages 199 to 202 of my *Mind Invaders* anthology. Despite the fact that I often dwell on my poverty in the introductions to books, very few of my readers suffer from the kind of misplaced human sympathy that leads them to send me £100 or even £10. I'm therefore forced to resort to cheap tricks like placement to rake in the ackers that enable me to seek mystic inspiration from the bottom of a bottle of Springbank. Please do rush out and buy a copy of *Mind Invaders,* it's an excellent book. Likewise, you really do need to purchase a hogshead of Springbank, you won't find a better malt and last time I checked the prices started at a mere £850. Write to Frank McHardy, General Manager, J & A Mitchell, Springbank Distillery, Campbeltown, Scotland PA26 6ET for full details about purchasing butts, hogsheads and barrels of both Springbank and Hazelburn. As the highly respected secondhand car salesman and literary figure Iain Sinclair once said to me, during the course of a particularly degenerate drinking session in a pub abutting a Jack The Ripper murder site: "Are you drunk?"

Personally I can't quite fathom the appeal of Hazelburn, I prefer Longrow, the other malt produced at the Springbank distillery. However, to return to the subject at hand, a number of my previously uncollected *Big Issue* articles have been gathered together in this book. These include 'Captive Of The KLF' (19 August 1996). This journalistic deception led to the arrest of Jimmy Cauty by Devon and Cornwall police. Cauty's detention was covered in detail by the *Western Morning News* (28 August 1996) in an article entitled 'Firearms Raid On A30 Star Home'. *The Big Issue* (4 November 1996) commented: "A spoof story in *Big Issue 195* on a stash of 'sonic weapons' stockpiled by former KLF star Jimmy Cauty prompted a raid on his home by anti-terrorist squad officers and dogs. Two of his tanks stationed at the Fairmile road protest site were removed for army inspection and Mr Cauty was taken to Exeter Police station and bailed until the end of the month."

It took the cops some time to realise they'd been had and, much to their embarrassment, the story stayed in circulation for several months. For example, John Duncan wrote in *The Guardian* (15 November 1996): "So where do you reckon the intelligence services get all their best stuff from? Telephone taps? High-level informers? Secret agents? Or none of the above? It appears in fact that they spend their days reading *The Big Issue*. Following an entirely spoofed article by self-styled 'art terrorist' Stewart Home describing how he was kidnapped and shown an arsenal of weapons at the house of KLF/K Foundation money-burner-in-chief Jim Cauty, Mr Cauty's abode was put under police surveillance for several days. Not long after, it was raided by 30 officers who searched the gaff from top to bottom and found nothing except two Saracen armoured cars which Mr Cauty keeps in his garden so as not to be underdressed at local road protests. Both are properly taxed and insured. Mr Cauty was released without charge."

Aside from the opportunities it offers for boozing, one of the things that attracts me to journalism is the diversity of the readership addressed by the popular press. The bizarre reactions of both Charlotte O'Sullivan and the Devon and Cornwall police to my work illustrates the diverse ways in which pieces of humorous journalism are sometimes understood. Obviously it is very easy to say too much in an introduction and as a consequence unnecessarily restrict the ways in which what follows is read. Rather than offering verities for the faithful, I prefer to construct texts with an internal tension and in this way I hope readers are encouraged to appropriate whatever they want from my work. While it might be possible to provide a superficially rational explanation of what has been collected here, this would entail laying off the Springbank for several hours, possibly even a whole day. Consequently, I refuse to indulge those who wish to construct themselves as bourgeois subjects with fripperies such as perspective, logic or sense. Make of this book what you will. All things are nothing to me.

Stewart Home
London
1 April 1999

BILL AND JIMMY MUTILATE A COW

BILL DRUMMOND AND JIMMY CAUTY were never happy being pop stars. After topping the charts with the KLF in the early nineties, the duo found themselves caught up in an escalating spiral of hype. To frustrate the expectations of their fans, they not only destroyed their musical career, but the money they'd earned from it – they burnt £1 million in £50 notes on the remote Scottish island of Jura – leaving them free to pursue myriad low-key projects.

Drummond co-wrote the novel *Bad Wisdom* with Mark 'Zodiac Mindwarp' Manning and embarked on a reading tour designed to blow away any pop star mystique that still clung to his persona. Suddenly the elusive character was accessible. The media ignored the book and Drummond's trek around the UK to promote it. Meanwhile, Cauty involved himself in the anti-roads protest movement, using a sound system mounted on an armoured car to bombard motorway contractors with mind bending white noise.

More recently, Bill and Jimmy were bidding against the likes of psychic spoon bender Uri Geller to buy the Rollright stone circle in rural Oxfordshire. Drummond and Cauty planned to conduct a series of rituals at the ancient monument, which is situated on a ley line, with the intention of overthrowing the British establishment. The owner, Pauline Flick, got wind of this and the duo's attempts at gazumping all comers were frustrated because some feared that their plans would result in the violent death of innumerable public figures.

Recently, Bill and Jimmy have heard rumours that the Government plans to sell off Stonehenge, and are determined to purchase it and use it for ritual purposes. To raise money for this project which, they say, will destroy the state, the duo are making music again after a five year break. Drummond and Cauty's first 2K performance was at the Barbican on 17 September. The hall was packed with trendy young artists, rock hipsters and leading occult figures.

The Barbican show premiered a new version of the KLF classic *What Time Is Love?* featuring a brass band and new lyrics built around the slogan 'Fuck The Millennium'. Bill and Jimmy scootered about the stage in motorised wheelchairs, mutilating a dead swan that symbolised the monarchy. As the show went on they were joined by a picket line of placard waving striking Liverpool dockers. At the end everyone in the audience was presented with a 'Fuck The Millennium' T-shirt, bag, poster and bumper sticker.

After the show, those in the know gathered on the corner of Commercial and Hanbury Streets in Spitalfields. A couple of hookers were soliciting business; their offer of straight sex for £20 at a nearby the Jack The Ripper murder site aroused a certain amount of interest. After a long wait several coaches arrived to convey us to the iron age Madmarston Hill Fort in Oxfordshire. The site lies on the powerful ley line that runs between the ancient Arbury Camp and the neolithic Rollright Stones.

On arrival at Madmarston the specially invited guests were confronted by a dead cow that was tied to a crucifix and illuminated by a spotlight. Behind this there was a huge billboard emblazoned with the words "Yes, Yes". Richard Essex of the Anti-Millennium Alliance kicked off the second part of the evening's events with a talk entitled *No Third Reich, No Third Millennium*. The nub of this speech was a proposal that we should abandon the Christian calendar and thus delay the arrival of the millennium for another six hundred years.

"In the past," Essex informed us, "revolutionaries have inaugurated new dating systems from the point at which the ancient regime collapsed, but this strikes me as being too egotistical. The Anti-Millennium Alliance proposal means adopting a calendar which is already nearly four hundred years old. It derives from the ancient Egyptian calendar and we call it the Modern Khemetic Calendar because Khem is a name for Egypt. The ancient Egyptians had a civil calendar which rotated over a 1,460 year cycle. The current cycle commenced in AD 1599. This coincides with the inauguration of the modern era in the realm of science. Thus we have reached the year 398 in the Modern Khemetic Calendar."

Richard Essex further confused his listeners by explaining the relationship between the Khemetic Calendar and various solar events, such as the rising of the star Sirius in the Canis Major constellation. At the end of the Anti-Millennium Alliance talk, everyone was shuffled around. There were mumbles of complaint when people realised that important music business figures had been assembled around the crucified cow, while everyone else was kept well back by a small army of assistants.

Then, amid bursts of excruciating white noise, Bill and Jimmy emerged from the shadows wearing protective clothing, gas masks and wielding axes above their heads. The duo quickly butchered the crucified cow, simultaneously splattering the assembled record company personnel with blood. Next, Drummond and Cauty scooped up great handfuls of offal and threw it around. A taped announcement informed everyone that those individuals who'd been splashed by gore would be held back, so that they could wipe themselves down with union flags. There was, we were told, a good chance the industry insiders had been infected with Mad Cow Disease. They travelled home on a separate coach from the rest of us!

When I spoke to Drummond on the phone the next day he explained it had been extremely difficult obtaining the dead cow: "I had to offer some slaughterhouse workers an enormous bribe. With the furore over BSE every farm animal has to be accounted for and the bodies disposed of in a strictly regulated fashion." Bill wasn't worried by the legal implications of his actions. "People are very angry about what we did, but the establishment wants to hush it up. We won't be prosecuted, the publicity around a court case would screw up all the diplomatic efforts that have gone into rehabilitating the image of British beef."

First published in *D>Tour*, October 1997

GETTING OFF ON BOOKS

I'VE LONG SUSPECTED that some of my more unsavoury acquaintances were getting their porno kicks from art. You won't find these characters doing the five knuckle shuffle over top-shelf material purchased from a newsagent. They prefer the intellectual atmosphere of bookshops and art galleries, where they can get their jollies while simultaneously boosting their social standing.

Since many middle-class men see art as a vehicle for sexual gratification, there are plenty of booksellers with lurid tales to tell about their customers. Marc Jackson spoke to me about a few of his more bizarre experiences in the trade. "When I worked at Foyles a middle-aged man was arrested for masturbating in the art section. He had some kind of arrangement with a piece of string. There was another guy who'd come in with a stick-on mirror that he'd put on his shoe, so that he could look up women's skirts. He was known to the security and we had to call them and get him chucked out if we saw him. The clientele were even worse when I was employed at Waterstones in the Brompton Road, the painter Francis Bacon was always coming in and trying to chat up members of staff."

Even the left-wing booksellers I spoke to said they'd experienced problems with customers getting off on the material they stocked. Richard Essex who now runs Unpopular Books told me: "When I worked at Rising Free we had one middle-aged man who came in regularly wanting lesbian material. He'd be panting as he asked for it. He used to buy stuff put out by the feminist Robin Morgan." It's certainly my experience that I'm more likely to have people trying to pick me up when I'm browsing in radical bookshops. Generally this isn't a case of attempts at horizontal recruitment, although there are Trotskyite groups who believe that you can sleep your way to political correctness.

Although the art and medical sections are those most likely to attract problematic customers, no bookshop department is safe. *The Bible* contains so many lewd passages that theology is best avoided. Likewise, philosophy and psychology pull in some particularly kinky characters. One disgraced professor is said to haunt bookshops offering members of the opposite sex 'lectures' on the problems of sense perception. His teaching technique is an unusual variant on the traditional table routine, often used in college seminars as a concrete example of an object whose appearance varies depending upon how one interacts with it. The colour of a table changes according to what kind of light falls upon it, while the amount of pressure applied when it is touched creates variations in how it feels. The disgraced academic allegedly uses his sexual organ as a means of illustrating these points.

The bizarre link between books and perverse behaviour is so well established that it has even manifested itself in art forms. London-based Paul Noble creates images of deviant behaviour involving books. "I did my first book drawing in 1992," Noble explains in a thick Geordie accent. "I found the smell of books would induce bowel movements but there are hardly ever toilets in bookshops or libraries. So I'd do a picture of someone having a dump in a book. It was a meeting of the animal and the intellectual. Like most artists, I'm just a total voyeur. Although I wouldn't want to masturbate in a library, people can understand it as the subject matter of a drawing. My mum couldn't get her head around the abstract paintings I did at college, so after I left I thought I'd make representational pictures she could recognise as art."

Noble's pictures appear positively sedate in comparison to the illustrious Jerry Dreva, who during the seventies became notorious as "the man who had a thousand orgasms for art." This was as a result of *Wanks For The Memories: The Seminal Works/Books Of Jerry Dreva,* which were made by the artist soaking erudite tomes with his own semen.

Cynics are perhaps justified when they suggest that artists are more interested in money than exploring sexuality. Sex will shift almost any product and stringent obscenity laws simply add to the frisson of naughtiness that fuels the demand for 'erotica'. Manchester police are currently examining two books by the photographer David Hamilton. While the legal issues raised by the Hamilton case are complex, one doesn't need to know much about aesthetics to reject his soft-focus pictures as naff. Nevertheless, Hamilton might like to try his luck by applying for a show at the East End community gallery Camerawork.

A diatribe against the 'puerile' fantasies of the Camerawork exhibitions organiser John Roberts can be found in the current issue of *Art Monthly.* Celia Cherm paraphrases an article on young British art by Roberts thus: "Imagine this bird, right, who's dead sexy, dead attractive, bawdy even – and she's into football. And she's gagging for it, right?" According to Roberts in his *Notes On 90s Art,* the imaginary young woman is typical of a new generation of artists. To me, she's more indicative of the way in which a growing number of professional men use aesthetics as a justification for consuming what is basically porn. Personally, I'd rather go and purchase something from the top-shelf of my local newsagent. It's more honest.

First published in *The Big Issue 214,* 6-12 January 1997

THE TOTAL ART OF C. JOHN TAYLOR

AMID ALL THE ARGUMENTS about what constitutes the avant-garde and whether it still exists, there are those who have assimilated many of the more advanced cultural forms of the past century and adapted them to some quite unlikely ends. While too much has been made of Malcolm McLaren's alleged recuperation of situationist theory while managing the Sex Pistols, there is still a great deal to be said about 84-year-old C. John Taylor's appropriation of Dada and Fluxus.

Taylor is the impresario behind the Highland Arts Studios. This pioneering retail operation has been at the cutting edge of the tartan tourist trade since the sixties. Taylor has shops in Luss, Oban, Callander, Inveraray and Easdale. His Highland Arts Studios provide tourists with cheap and nasty souvenirs of their Scottish holidays. There are tea-towels, plates and prints featuring the work of self-styled 'artist, poet, composer' C. John Taylor, all executed in an atrocious naive realist style. The subject matter ranges from the Highland landscape to 'great' men and women. Among the latter one finds Charlie Chaplin, Robert Burns, Elizabeth II, Winston Churchill, Shakespeare, Mother Teresa and television personalities such as Russell Harty. Taylor is also inordinately fond of beauty contest winners, girls in bikinis and sickly religious themes.

The 'traditional Highland welcome' awaiting Taylor's fans consists of shop assistants shoving trays of shortbread at potential customers. The Highland Arts Studios butter tablet ranks among the worst I have ever tasted, while Taylor's chocolate eclair sweets are the perfect present for people you don't like. Within minutes of entering Taylor's Isle Of Seil shop and consuming a few of these 'treats', I felt sick. The fact that Taylor thought it worth informing his customers that the Highland Arts Exhibition I'd come to see is "advertised in the *Sunday Post*" was not reassuring. Taylor also advertises in the *Oban Times* and I'm sure he'd pay for space in the *Sunday Sport* or *Weekly World News* if he thought it would pull in the punters. In his use of the mass media Taylor comes across as a low budget copy of the futurist F. T. Marinetti. The latter paid for 'The Founding and Manifesto of Futurism 1909' to appear as an advert on the front page of *Le Figaro.*

When I visited the Highlands Art Exhibition several of Taylor's canvases were obscured by novelty gifts and other tat. Taylor doesn't sell his 'original' works, he simply exploits their potential for reproduction. Likewise, Taylor has set a number of his poems to 'waltz time melodies' and hearing *Islands Of Beauty* played repeatedly in his shop gave me a headache. This Scots flavoured song features a passage recited by Taylor in an incongruous north of England accent. Various recordings of Taylor's works were available. The level of his sincerity and attention to detail can be gleaned from the fact that the sleeve of *The Loch Lomond Song* claims it was "written beside 'the bonny bonny banks o' Loch Lomond'" while the label states it was "composed on Seil Island." Likewise, while Taylor attributes the similarities between his work and the famous folk song *Loch Lomond* to coincidence, I would ascribe it to cynicism.

Before turning to 'art' Taylor made a fortune as a salesman, and the fact that he is able to sell his prodigious output of paintings in the form of reproductions on Highland souvenirs demonstrates that his skills still lie principally in the realm of commerce. Taylor's homespun philosophy is simple: stack 'em high and sell 'em cheap. There are endless special offers at the Highlands Arts Studios, two copies of his *'Ten Of The Best' Poems* for the price of one, a strategy that has no doubt boosted the much trumpeted seventy thousand plus sales of this £1 a shot pamphlet. While John Betjeman appears to be Taylor's poetic model, his work is actually closer to Scotland's alternative national bard William McGonagall. Just as McGonagall's inept handling of rhyme and metre in *The Tay Bridge Disaster* transformed a Victorian tragedy into farce, Taylor did something similar for late seventies politics with his poem *Margaret Thatcher*. Taylor concludes this Tory nursery rhyme with the words: "Our need is desperately/For a vote catcher!!/God bless God for sending/Mrs. Margaret Thatcher!!"

However, perhaps even more remarkable than Taylor's works are the photographs of the man that appear on many Highland Arts Studios products. With his black rimmed spectacles, goatee beard and cap, Taylor comes across as a caricature of a modern painter. It is almost as if the 'poet, artist, composer' modelled himself on Tony Hancock's satiric deconstruction of avant-garde iconoclasm in the film *The Rebel*. Photographs of Taylor often show him with a paint brush in his hand, and another in his mouth. Even more amusing are pictures that show Taylor, the canvass he is working on and his model. Invariably, the painting and the subject bear only a cursory resemblance to each other.

In Taylor's Oban shop I came across a sealed plastic container with lots of numbered yellow lumps inside. I imagined that this was a Fluxus-style art piece until an assistant explained the numbers that jiggled onto a small ledge would provide me with a lucky lottery combination. This modest work was almost lost amid a nightmare array of gifts in tartan, souvenir pens and tacky ornaments. An eerie silence hung over the shop and an older assistant asked her younger colleague if the tape machine was broken. "Unfortunately not," was the deadpan response. The elderly saleswoman immediately made her way to the tape player and split-seconds later Taylor's waltz time melodies were booming from the beat box. Like sixties iconoclasts such as the Fluxus artist Ben Vautier, Taylor has created a total environment in which punters can experience his total art.

It has been suggested that the aim of the classical avant-garde was the integration of art and life. While it is doubtful that the

Dadaists would have viewed shopping as a medium for realising this ambition, not even they could deny that Taylor is an innovator when it comes to the hard sell. The situationist Guy Debord wrote in his book *The Society Of The Spectacle* that: "Tourism, human circulation considered as consumption, a by-product of the circulation of commodities, is fundamentally nothing more than the leisure of going to see what has already become banal." In his cynical exploitation of the tartan tourist trade, a megalomaniac like Taylor provides a perfect illustration of this dictum. Taylor shares the concerns of the avant-garde but he has reversed its ideological perspective. Rather than being a critic of commodity culture, he is an advocate of conspicuous consumption.

Previously unpublished

Royal Watch:
Sex, smack and satanism

ANYONE WHO THINKS that the disintegration of various royal marriages endangers the monarchy, simply doesn't understand where the Queen's real power lies. Elizabeth Windsor is the richest woman on the earth and depriving this parasite of a formal role within the British state would have a less than negligible effect on her ability to control world affairs. The Queen doesn't need to waste time on Westminster. Lizzie's incredible wealth gives her the power to bankrupt any state that attempts to resist her evil will.

For the past two centuries, the bulk of the royal family's liquid assets have been invested in drug, gold and diamond operations. Most of the trading practices in which the monarchy is involved became illegal during the course of this century – but this doesn't bother the Windsors, since they never need to get their hands dirty. All the dope dealing and related activities are carried out for the royals by their loyal cadre within The Order Of St John.

Many people have been duped into believing that the Knights of Malta are chiefly concerned with running the St John Ambulance Brigade. This operation with its HQ at St Johns Gate, Clerkenwell, is simply a front. While there is circumstantial evidence that various royals have used the norman crypt of the Grand Priory Church for the purpose of ritual child abuse, we have to look to the Mall – and not Clerkenwell – if we're to find the puppet-masters who are pulling the strings on world affairs.

The important members of the Order of St John are not those who've innocently entered the lower echelons of this sinister organisation through volunteer work, but the men who run the financial institutions that make up the City of London and its counterparts in the United States and Canada. This Anglo-American elite invests the royal family's funds and then launders the billions in profits that come back from innumerable illegal trading operations. It was with this end in mind that Queen Victoria granted the revived British Knights of Malta a royal charter in 1888 and installed the ruling sovereign as the head of this 'chivalistic' order.

While the Queen acts as titular head of the anglican church, she is secretly active in an ancient pagan cult. For years, Prince Charles has been preparing himself to undertake the first properly occult reign since his mother's namesake, Elizabeth I, ruled this country with the assistance of John Dee. Efforts to realise this ambition are at the root of the prince's marital problems. Lady Di had to be coerced into participating in various sex magick rituals after tying the wedding knot. Charles wanted a 'moonchild' as his heir and blames his wife's lack of co-operation in occult matters for the failure of rituals designed to achieve this end. Lady Di's alleged 'suicide attempts' were, in fact, the result of psychic attacks directed against her by the Queen Mother, who had sided with her grandson on this matter. Luckily for Diana, members of the Archaeogeodetic Association were able to save her from death with the aid of some very powerful white magick.

Investigations by the London Psychogeographical Association have revealed that the recent turmoil in the royal family is largely due to the building of the Canary Wharf Tower. The building stands on a ley line that runs through Chislehurst Caves and St Annes Church in Limehouse, via the Queen's House in Greenwich, to All Saints Church in Blackheath (where Terry Waite made his BBC World Service Broadcast after the end of his faked 'ordeal' as a Middle East hostage). Interestingly, the Bridge Room in the Queens House contains copies of paintings depicting the 1565 Seige of Malta that were executed by the same artist who did the originals that are housed in the Chamber of the Grand Master of the Knights of St John.

Once the royals realised that the Canary Wharf Tower was soaking up all the power from the ley line which they'd been using to nourish their occult activities, they went on the attack and bankrupted Olympia and York who'd been developing the site. However, this didn't stop the Tower from throwing the ancient earth energies – which the monarchy had been perverting to evil uses – out into space. Liz then sent out the order that Canary Wharf should be blown up in a fake 'IRA' bomb outrage. Fortunately, members of the Order Of St Thomas – whose patron saint was cruelly murdered by the British monarchy hundreds of years ago – managed to foil this plot with a very deft piece of white magic. According to researchers from the Neoist Alliance, Liz and her offspring are now planning to tap into other ancient powers by ritually slaughtering hundreds of children. The first of an involved series of rituals is due to commence at dusk on the spring equinox.

First published in *Underground 1,* Spring 1993

A REPORT ON PSYCHOGEOGRAPHICAL SEX IN SCOTLAND

DURING THE COURSE of several field trips to Scotland, I experienced strong orgasms in a good number of ancient structures. I was very pleasantly surprised by the potency of orgasm achieved at Carn Liath, Strathsteven, which is in the 'Guardianship' of the Secretary of State for Scotland and very easily accessible, being located on the coastal side of the A9, or the 'Great Road North' as it is known locally. During my visit, the nearby car parking area was full of holiday-makers enjoying picnics. One elderly Yorkshire woman asked me if I'd been to Dunrobin Castle but showed no interest in the well-signed broch, and my glamorous assistant and I were lucky enough to have it to ourselves. While we were in the structure, a twenty-something couple ran across the A9 towards the broch, but then swerved around it and made their way to the beach. The walls of this defensive structure shielded me from view and a blow job resulted in a swift but intense orgasm.

More oral led to a slower but equally potent ejaculation screened from observation by the round wall of the Cairn o' Get. Although this tomb at Garrywhin is well signed from the main road, there is barely space for three small cars in the parking area. It is then a bit of a walk to the cairn. Chattering from the path alerted me to a couple approaching and, mission accomplished, I adjusted my clothing – leaving the site free for the pleasurable enjoyment of others. The Grey Cairns of Camster number among the most famous attractions of the Caithness region but I found them disappointing. The restored roofing in the chambers of Camster Long is obtrusive and very poorly done. It didn't surprise me to discover that both the cairns and the large house that stands in the eight acres of boggy ground surrounding them were up for sale at £150,000. Results were mixed at the Hill o' Many Stanes, with my female assistant finding the ambience created by the rows of about 200 small stones more erotically charged than me.

Although busy during the day, one can enjoy the ruins of the five thousand year old village of Skara Brae for free after the official closing time under the light of the Orkney simmer dim. I arrived at the famous tourist attraction late one bright June evening to discover a crusty couple shagging in the otherwise deserted complex. Skara Brae was delightful but I preferred the ambience of the Pictish and Norse remains at the Brough of Birsay, where sex would have been possible if I'd been up for staying in the ruined village during the hours it is cut off from the Orkney mainland by the sea. The Brough of Deerness was quite deserted when I visited – and provided an excellent site for penetrative sex on a bright summer's day. Maes Howe is locked up at night, so possibilities for sex inside the tomb are limited – hit and run blow jobs might be possible if your timing is good. I didn't manage anything at all.

While both the Stones of Stenness and Ring of Brodgar on Orkney attract prodigious numbers of visitors, nearly all of them arrive by car, coach or motorcycle, so rampant sex is possible if your timing is good. The warning sound of engines provides ample opportunities for the adjustment of clothing should you consider this necessary. The best times for sex are later on in the evening. I found the Stones of Stenness the more ambient site, although the sheep shit which surrounds them was somewhat hazardous. The reconstructed Barnhouse village nearby was even more erotically charged than Skara Brae. Likewise, the field which is the former site of the Ring of Bookan – unsigned and largely ignored by tourists – is nevertheless very sexually potent. This site is overlooked by a farmhouse, so caution is advised, although full penetrative sex is easy to perform here without being disturbed once it gets dark.

I found sex in the recumbent stone circles of the Grampian Region produced particularly intense orgasms. One of the best preserved recumbent circles is Easter Aquorthies and although the site is relatively exposed, my assistant gave me a quick blow job before another couple arrived to contemplate the ancient stones. Loanhead Of Daviot stone circle and cremation cemetery is screened by trees to the south and east making daylight sex easier. However, the local scout hut is situated beneath some of these trees, so psychogeographers should check to make sure no children are playing in the woods before engaging in sex. More remote, better shielded and currently unsigned is the Nine Stanes of Mulloch stone circle in Forestry Commission woodland three-and-a-half miles south-east of Banchory. My investigations revealed that female orgasms were particularly strong at this site. I enjoyed particularly good sex at the Achavanich megalithic horseshoe by Lock Stemster in Caithness, and the nearby Guidebest stone circle situated at the edge of the Latheron Wheel Burn. Even more extraordinary were my orgasms at the Sunhoney and Tyrebagger recumbent stone circles.

One of the most puissant sites I visited was the Learable Hill complex at the Strath of Kildonan. My assistant and I approached the Learable Hill from Helmsdale village by the single track A897. The road runs alongside the River Helmsdale. There are no signs directing the curious to the stone circles, stone rows, standing stones or cairns. Indeed, the rickety footbridge across the river to the strip of land allowing public access to the site is often closed on the grounds that it is unsafe! The Helmsdale Tourist Information Office told me that it was impossible to get to the Learable Hill because the footbridge across to it had been dismantled after being declared unsafe.

When I replied that I would wade across the river to access the site, a phone call was made to the local gillie who gave detailed instructions on how to get across safely.

Previously published in *Sleaze Nation, Vol. 2 no. 5,* 16 April 1998

SLOW CHOCOLATE AUTOPSY

HACKNEY BASED NOVELIST IAIN SINCLAIR is well known for his psychogeographical surveys of London. Over the course of thirty years he's written about everywhere from swinging Shoreditch through to the badlands of Tilbury. Sinclair's work is an endless mapping and remapping, remixing and recontexualising of a city in constant flux. Incapable of adhering to the made-to-measure standards of the publishing industry, he mixes fiction with reportage, poetry with film-making. Sinclair is forever bringing people together, putting on exhibitions and readings, then sitting back to enjoy the incomprehension with which an expectant public greets the creative madness of his protégés. The publication of his latest book *Slow Chocolate Autopsy* (Phoenix House £9.99), a collaboration with comic artist Dave McKean, was marked by an evening of readings that were bizarre even by Sinclair's unruly standards.

Prior to the launch I'd already experienced some severe weirdness while being filmed for scenes in *The Falconer*, the Channel 4 extravaganza Sinclair is currently making with fellow novelist Chris Petit. In Bishopsgate we were grilled by armed cops who mistook us for a team of terrorists monitoring their security set-up. After the lead actress disappeared from her Hackney Road bedsit, I was brought back in to spout conspiracy theories about this to Petit's girlfriend Emily. Needless to say, Sinclair expected me to invent new and utterly unbelievable stories from minute to minute. He wanted everyone from Princess Di through to underground film-maker Peter Whitehead libelled. In the midst of this craziness, I blithely agreed to participate in the events being planned around the publication of Sinclair's new book.

I'd done Sinclair launches before and he usually booked some low-life venue, then put me on immediately after Kathy Acker. The setting for the *Slow Chocolate Autopsy* shindig was a decommissioned public toilet in Spitalfields. Acker wasn't around, having moved back to the States after announcing she'd lost interest in post-modernism. So instead of back to back readings in which gender is deconstructed through an examination of stereotyped male and female roles, Sinclair teamed me up with performance artist Joyce Grant. This post-porn modernist wanted to suck me off while I read a passage from my novel *Defiant Pose* which features a skinhead reciting from a book whilst being given a blow job.

As I started reading Joyce knelt in front of me and unzipped my Levi's. I had my head spot-lit but there was no other illumination. Grant was geared up in black clothing and a murmur rippled through the crowd as people realised what was going on. Joyce shook my dick to make it hard but I tried not to pay any attention to what she was doing. I just concentrated on the words I was reciting. During rehearsals I'd found that if I really focused my mind, I was able to proceed with the reading even when I was ejaculating. What I hadn't counted on was a disturbance at the door. A tramp wandered in thinking the venue was still a public toilet. After he started urinating on the steps, a fight broke out. I stumbled over my words but no one really noticed. Although I failed to complete the recitation from my novel, I did at least enjoy a healthy orgasm.

After the hobo had been ejected, Peter Whitehead got up to give a talk. For years rumours have circulated to the effect that he is an MI5 man. Whitehead dismissed this suggestion by saying that everywhere he went people assumed he was a spook because twenty-five years ago he'd driven around Pakistan in a Landrover purchased from the British army. Apparently, even the CIA were taken in by this scam and protected Whitehead without realising he was actually fronting an international operation to smuggle falcon's eggs. Whitehead then proceeded to speak about everything from his sixties documentary films through to Sinclair and Petit's upcoming Channel 4 special about him and a recent novel exposing intelligence involvement in the publishing industry. Other subjects covered included his bondage photographs and ongoing obsession with the occult. Whitehead described how, after he'd performed an occult ritual at the Callanish stone circle last year, a UFO was spotted nearby and many other anomalous phenomena were reported.

Sinclair was up next showcasing some brand new poetry that imitates the patter of secondhand book dealers: "BROWN, Wenzell. *Monkey On My Back (Teen-Agers Caught in the Dope Racket).* PB original WDL, 1958. Junkies blasting for thrills – the menace of teen-age drug addiction. Striking pictorial wrappers, somewhat rubbed and creased. About VG. £6.50. THE FAMOUS AMERICAN WRITER (ie M. L. 'Tony' Lowes). *Elephant Book (Or How The Elephant Made It Through The Psychedelic Symbol)* Albion Village Press 1971. Illustrated thru by Tim Goulding. Cannabis leaf design endpapers. Jail journals, drug tourism, visions. Cloth bound, numbered and signed. Fine. £15.00. DRUMMOND, Bill & MANNING, Mark. *Bad Wisdom (The Lighthouse At The Top Of The World).* 1996 uncorrected proof copy. Yellow wrappers. Ex-KLF art guerrilla Drummond and Zodiac Mindwarped Manning set off in general direction of North Pole to 'sacrifice an icon of Elvis Presley.' A loud salute to 'bad craziness' in Finland. Alcohol, pornography, nightmare, snow, (Ms Smilla would never believe it). Fine. £25.00."

There was another disturbance when an emotional emissary from the *Modern Review* failed to grasp the fictional nature of Sinclair's absurdist poetry and after hearing the description "obscure American cult figure achieves a new record in name dropping" became desperate to acquire Jay Landesman's *Jaywalking.* Sinclair abandoned the stage in disgust, leaving us in the capable hands of Chris Petit doing a DJ thing. The toilet began to empty, the free booze had run out, and in the face of this calamity not even space-age easy listening could hold the attention of those freeloaders present. However, Petit proved that he knew his stuff by playing both Elektrik Cokernut's *Jungle Juice* and the Rockridge Synthesizer Orchestra's cover of *Get Off My Cloud*. All things considered, it was a top night.

First published in *D>Tour*, November 1997

TOWARDS AN ACOGNITIVE CULTURE

Henry Flynt in conversation with Stewart Home, New York, 8 March 1989.

HENRY FLYNT was born in Greensboro, North Carolina, in 1940. In 1961, after his New York debut in Yoko Ono's Chambers Street loft, he originated the idea of concept art. Then, in 1962, Flynt initiated a utopian critique of art from the stand-point of the absolute subjectivity of taste. He destroyed most of his early works, left the art world and began a campaign to 'demolish serious culture.'

During the seventies Flynt returned to college to take a phd in communist economics. In 1987 he resumed making concept art in conjunction with the crystallisation of his researches into the foundations of science. Flynt now views his previous assessment of art as being heavily conditioned by the period in which he entered the New York art scene. Nevertheless, his critique provides a useful starting point for discussing the class basis of culture. As the eighties draw to a close, Flynt's extreme utopianism is gaining currency among a younger generation of thinkers (particularly those who emerged from the now defunct Neoist movement). Simultaneously, his recent work is creating ripples of interest among the cognoscenti of the official art world.

The principal collection of Flynt's writings is *Blueprint For A Higher Civilisation* (Multhipla Edizioni, Milan 1975). A recent essay on concept art by Flynt and an interview with him can by found in *Io 41* edited by Charles Stein (North Atlantic Books, Berkeley 1988).

This interview took place in a sandwich bar on the corner of Broadway and Spring, a few yards away from the Emily Harvey Gallery where Flynt's 'Classic Modernism and Authentic Concept Art' was on show. It is chiefly concerned with Flynt's activities during the sixties and his utopian critique of art.

Home: How did your ideas develop, what direction were you coming from in the early sixties?

Flynt: My early work was philosophic, what would be called epistemology, I was convinced I'd discredited cognition. When somebody says that all statements are false, the obvious problem is that as an assertion it's self-defeating. I had to find a way to frame this insight which was not self-defeating and that's in *Blueprint*, the essay entitled 'The Flaws Underlying Beliefs.' One has to do what Wittgenstein claimed to do in the *Tractatus Logico-Philosophicus*, which is to use the ladder and then throw it away. The way I devolved, moved out from, this position of strict cognitive nihilism, was with the idea of building a new culture which would depart profoundly from the scientific culture in which we live.

I was a student at Harvard and that's where I learned about so called avant-garde music. Jackson Pollock, abstract expressionism and action painting were well known at this time, but the music was more of a cult thing with individual composers doing very unusual work. It was very hard to find out about what these people were doing. I was told that people like Cage were the latest thing. Christian Wolff, who was an associate of Cage, was at Harvard as a graduate student and there were a lot of concerts of so called avant-garde music held at the university.

Home: How did you got involved with the set promoting this type of music?

Flynt: I was trying to be up with the latest thing. To a point I just took what I was offered, logical positivism in philosophy and the so called avant-garde in music. I began composing works which were imitative of the music I was being told about. I was also very interested in translating the music into visual terms. At the same time I felt a tremendous disquiet about the avant-garde; there was something very inauthentic about it. There was the mystique of scientificity – Stockhausen was making claims which were actually false, that were philosophically discreditable. Another thing that happened was that when I came to New York I began to meet the people who became the most famous artists of our time. I was insecure about my own level of ability, I didn't know whether I could compete with these people and, at the same time, I was wondering what is this anyway? I felt very uneasy about the fact that all these people were competing with each other to become rich and famous, and the original reason for all this activity had been lost.

Home: So it was when you came into contact with the people composing this music that you became critical of it.

Flynt: When I began competing with the other artists in New York. Also, at that time, I discovered classical North Indian music. I spent a lot of time with this and began to question the whole enterprise of classical music as such. I have a lot of problems with modern European culture. I find European music to be very four-square; it really lends itself to computerisation. In classical oil painting, there seemed to be a radical turn to seeing things as the camera sees them, with that technological modification. I began to have a tremendous problem with all of this. At the same time I was listening to black music and I began to think that the best musicians were receiving the worst treatment. The people who were doing the greatest work were despised as lower class, with no dignity accorded to what they did, while the stuff being promoted as serious culture and performed in the Lincoln Centre was absolutely worthless. There was no real emotion in it; the possibility of ingenuous experience had been replaced by an ideology of science and scientism.

I became very angry about the fact that I'd been talked into going to these Cage concerts when I was in college, that I'd sat and tried to make myself like that stuff and think in those terms. I felt I'd been brainwashed, that it was a kind of damage to my sensibilities. I'm still mad about this, I still feel I've not recovered from the experience.

Home: How was this anger expressed in your activities during the early sixties?

Flynt: At that time I was initiating concept art. I was doing a lot of things, many of them imitative. The purpose of concept art as a genre is to unbrainwash our mathematical and logical faculties. At the same time it's bound up with aesthetic delectation. I think these two aspects are integral to concept art. It's not just an artificial pasting together of the two things, they actually change each other in the course of their interaction.

From there I moved to an absolutely subjective position aesthetically, where each individual should become aware of their unformed taste. I used the term 'brend' to signify this, and thought that it would replace art. Basically, at this time, I viewed any work of art as an imposition of another person's taste and saw the individual making this imposition as a kind of dictator. I don't think there's any irony about the fact that I was beginning to dabble in political leftism at the very time I was inventing a theory in which art disappears and is replaced by a kind of absolute individualism. It's not strange if you understand what the final utopia of socialism was supposed to be. It's no different from talking about getting rid of money or the state.

It was then that I began demonstrating against serious culture. In hindsight, the actual course of events has been very humiliating for me because no one picked up on the intellectual critique I made of Stockhausen. Another point I made was that black American music was a new language, and I don't feel this was ever really acknowledged. What happened was that rock became an incredible commercial success; people just became bored with serious music and it was forgotten. It was not an intellectual battle or a battle of principle at all.

34

Home: How was the group Action Against Cultural Imperialism organised?

Flynt: It wasn't, the organisation didn't exist, it was just a bluff.

Home: You didn't hold policy meetings?

Flynt: No. There were two stages to this affair. At first we were demonstrating against all serious culture. The organisation was really just me and Tony Conrad. At that time Tony was living with Jack Smith, who just came along with us. At first he didn't want to do it, he told us he had work in the Museum of Modern Art and that he wouldn't picket them. Then I got out the signs that I'd made for the demonstration and he began giggling hysterically. He ended up coming along because he thought it was funny. The focus changed tremendously as my interest in politics developed. I was meeting people who were calling my attention to issues of socialism, which I'd never really thought about.

Home: Who were these people?

Flynt: You wouldn't know them, somebody named Richard Ohmann, he's an English professor today. I converted myself to Marxism through reading. The Cuban revolution had just taken place and there was a tremendous discussion going on about it, there were books coming out on the subject. I got into it in that way and by 1964 I was affiliated with a Marxist group. The focus of the cultural demonstrations changed tremendously. I began to concentrate on the issues of race and imperialism. As a political statement the demonstrations were an absolute failure, nobody understood why I was holding them. I was told my activities were creating deep confusion about where I was coming from and why I was angry. The chairman of Workers World Party suggested I write a book. He said, you don't present a new theory at a demonstration, you write a book about it. That's how *Communists Must Give Revolutionary Leadership In Culture* came to be written.

Home: So this was in the mid-sixties?

Flynt: Yes, a lot of things were happening then. Around 1967 I began backing away from dogmatic Leninism, not so much because I thought it was false, I just decided there was nothing utopian about it. When you translate it from theory into practice it becomes just another political event[1].

Home: To return to the point about confusion, to me that seems central to what you do. Before we started taping the conversation, you said your writing was a black hole which would suck people in and deconstruct their mode of thought.

Flynt: That was in relation to cognition. I have a picture of an ideal consciousness which the writings are directed towards producing. It's not confused, I'm actually a great fan of lucidity.

Home: I wasn't implying that your formulations were confused, what I was trying to say was that the texts have a disorientating effect on the reader.

Flynt: I associate lucidity with belieflessness. I'm trying to assemble materials for a different mode of life, but it's a completely open question about how they might connect up. The whole drive of western culture, the part of it which is serious, is towards an extreme objectification. It's carried to the point where the human subject is treated almost as if it's dirt in the works of a watch. I'm trying to go to the source of this insane aberration, so that I can dissolve it. I want to do this by integrating subjectivity and objectivity, by making these two things intrinsically interdependent.

First published in *Smile 11,* Summer 1989

1. ie the modernisation strategy of last resort. cf 'The Three Levels Of Politics' in *Blueprint*. [Note added].

My quest for the Grail at Glastonbury

MY FRIENDS WERE HORRIFIED but no one was able to dissuade me. I had resolved to visit Glastonbury. If I had been in my early twenties it might have been put down to youthful folly, but I was approaching middle-age. What's more, I lived in East London and was the author of half a dozen novels that had achieved cult status thanks to the utterly excessive amounts of gratuitous sex 'n' violence I'd thrown into them. When I told people that I was doing research for a new book they'd look relieved, until I revealed that my subject matter was the Quest for the Holy Grail. Glastonbury has attracted its fair share of nutters over the years, a number of whom believed they had recovered the Grail, so I'd figured they'd provide some easy laughs in a comic novel. That said, it was amusing to watch the amount of revulsion the mere mention of Glastonbury induced in several otherwise very broadminded and level-headed individuals.

On arrival at Glastonbury I decided to check out the town, leaving the afternoon free to take in the sites favoured by the 'spiritually' inclined. The sheer number of hippie emporiums was in itself farcical, but a couple were particularly noteworthy. For fans of religious brain candy the British Orthodox shop is unmissable. It operates on the basis that the doctrines of Celtic and Orthodox Christianity are completely compatible since the heyday of the former predates the Great Schism of 1054 when Pope Leo IV and Michael Cerularius, patriarch of Constantinople, split the Christian church in two. The proprietor would have relieved me of a few quid if he'd been selling books or kitsch ornaments that fused Celtic and

37

Orthodox elements, but his stock was either one thing or the other. I thought about asking the black robed dude behind the counter whether he'd be geared up as a Celt if I came back later in the week. Unfortunately, he was a lot bigger than me and had been glowering as I sniggered at some particularly tacky display items, so I decided to keep my mouth shut.

The Goddess And The Green Man shop was devoted entirely to the male and female pagan archetypes. A mature earth mother browsing the shelves engaged me in conversation. She seemed to be wondering if I'd like to try a little Goddess worship with her. I complained I couldn't find the book I wanted. She unwittingly gave me my feeder line by asking what I'd hoped to buy. "The autobiography of Sex Pistols singer Johnny Rotten, the green-haired man of 1977," I replied deadpan. The woman was at least a dozen years older than me and she knew I was being sarcastic, so that was that. However, as I moved around the town I encountered more and more new age types who'd engage me in conversation. What particularly delighted me was the fact that several attractive girls in their early twenties either missed or didn't mind the ironic component in my banter. I was quickly convinced Glastonbury was a place I'd want to revisit – I appeared to have landed in pussy paradise.

After the shops, my next stop was the Tor. I took the longer and harder route up, enjoying the climb. It was windy at the top, but I sat down and admired the view along with a dozen other visitors. I then spent a few hours examining different parts of the hill. There is unusual terracing on the Tor in the shape of a distorted classical maze. Interested parties disagree over whether the maze was deliberately created as a religious processional route, is the result of medieval agricultural practices or merely a chance pattern caused by natural erosion. Despite these arguments, for the past thirty years the Tor has been recognised as boasting the largest maze in the world, so I wasn't going to leave Glastonbury without taking a good look at it. Eventually I made my way back into the town. After buying a drink and snack in Kwik Save, I headed for the bus stop.

"How long will I have to wait before I can catch a bus to Bristol?" a girl with a Californian accent enquired.

"There'll be one along in about five minutes."

"I'm into channelling, what are you into?"

"Avant-bardism," I replied.

"What's that?"

"When the ancient Celts went into battle," I explained, "they used to take their bards with them. The satire of the Celtic poets was so powerful that it is alleged it brought blisters to the cheeks of their opponents. The bards didn't need weapons because they were so adept at using their tongues. I'm trying to revive the art."

"But what use would it be?"

"I know some people who are being hassled by a gang of extraterrestrial teenagers and I want to help them."

The girl, who introduced herself as Ellie, followed me onto the bus and sat down beside me. Ellie had heard the Grail mentioned many times in the few days she'd stayed in Glastonbury but didn't know much about it, so she asked me if I had a detailed knowledge of the subject. I explained that there were two crucial objects in the medieval Grail romances and that she'd reap the greatest spiritual benefit by directing her attention towards the bleeding lance. When we got off the bus we found a B&B together. It wasn't long before I'd pulled Ellie's knickers down in order to view the object of my Quest. Not only did I know instinctively what this particular cup had been constructed to hold, I'd had the foresight to bring some condoms along so that I might serve the Grail safely. I'd convinced Ellie that I could initiate her into the arcane secrets of sex magick. No matter how ridiculous anything I might claim sounds, I can always find someone who'll believe it. Likewise, there are a lot more damaged girls where Ellie came from.

Previously unpublished

THE ANTIQUES ROADSHOW

THROUGHOUT THE SWINGING SIXTIES a good many young people imagined that they belonged to the first generation that could do anything, which mostly meant being a bohemian. Although no longer far out and fabulous, sixties has-beens still cling to the belief that it is possible to do one thing today, and another tomorrow. The sheer number of once beautiful people who've waddled onto the gallery circuit in recent years is proof of a tenacious, if largely misplaced, belief in their own creative capacities.

Thirty years ago, self-important groovy people like David Bowie and the recently dead Allen Ginsberg were inspired to mix different art forms by the burgeoning 'happenings' movement. More recently, mixed-media experimentation has given way to self-indulgence, with sixties stars attempting to revitalise their celebrity status through exhibitions of paintings. Most pop icons who've made credible art works did so at the height of their fame, through a marriage of music, theatre and painting. Attempts by former members of the glitterati to reinvent themselves as artists are rarely successful.

Sixties movie icon David Hemmings shot to fame when he starred in the Antonioni film *Blow Up*. This portrait of swinging London included a scene where a game of tennis was played without a ball. *Eclectic Similarities* by Hemmings, a solo art show which opens this week at London's Osborne Studio Gallery, promises to be considerably more pedestrian. Working in the highly traditional mediums of pen, pencil and water-colour, the faded luvvie now finds artistic inspiration in what Pimm's swilling toffs still call 'the season'. Occasionally broadening his horizons beyond Henley, Lord's, Ascot and Goodwood, Hemmings has also knocked out some London townscapes and a series of pictures on the theme of magic. However, it's with the storyboards from his film and TV production credits, including *The A Team,* that he finally manages to scrape the bottom of his threadbare barrel. Don't expect any surprises – Hemmings doesn't have it in him to fling a pot of paint in the public's face.

Infinitely superior to *Eclectic Similarities* is Brian Eno's current show *Music For White Cube,* running at London's White Cube gallery until 31 May. Eno being Eno, it comes as no surprise that there is nothing to see in this exhibition. Instead, there is a room of randomly generated 'ambient' music, something the former Roxy Music star pioneered in the late-sixties. In the words of White Cube, "the installation consists of four CD stations each playing a specially cut CD containing between eight and sixteen tracks. The CD players are set to 'shuffle' mode, thereby selecting tracks at random, to produce a landscape of sound that continually remakes itself."

Don't be put off by the po-faced promotion – the work is a lot more interesting than the press release implies. After all, Eno has a great sense of fun. He is rightly notorious for having relieved himself in the dadaist ready-made *Fountain* – an ordinary urinal that artist Marcel Duchamp signed R. Mutt and then submitted for exhibition.

Considerably less successful are the paintings and sculpture of Eno's fellow glam rocker David Bowie. Some of these were shown a couple of years ago under the title *New Afro/Pagan And Work 1975-1995* at Chertavia Fine Art in London. Bowie's pictures were a mixture of expressionistic squibs and fantasy figures set against an underlay of Laura Ashley wallcoverings. With his usual aplomb, Bowie admitted in the accompanying brochure "in neither music nor art have I a real style, craft or technique. I just plummet through on either a wave of euphoria or mind-splintering dejection."

Beyond the obvious financial rewards, one is left wondering

why Bowie bothers himself with creative matters. The same might be said of actor Tony Curtis, who is currently showing his sub-Cubist paintings in Cannes. The Berlin based art curator Berthold Golomstock is currently putting together an exhibition of social realist style paintings by original Stones guitarist Brian Jones, to be toured internationally in 1999.

Art exhibitions by long forgotten sixties stars are likely to become an increasingly common feature of the cultural landscape. Former teen icons suffering from middle-aged spread find painting landscapes on a Sunday afternoon a considerably less demanding pursuit than making innovative music and films.

First published in *The Big Issue 233*, 19–25 May 1997

ORGANISED CHAOS

The tabloids loathe them, but anarchists are too busy arguing with each other to riot.

ANARCHISM IS OFTEN ASSOCIATED WITH CHAOS and makes newspaper headlines whenever there's been a riot on the British mainland. The Anarchy In The UK festival, on all this week across London, demonstrates that the vast majority of anarchists aren't interested in throwing bricks and bottles at the police. While anarchism as a political doctrine has never exerted much influence outside Spain and the Ukraine, the impact of anarchist ideas on the arts has been enormous. Bohemianism is a quintessentially anarchist pursuit and it is this, principally in its subcultural guises, that forms the focus for the ten day Anarchy In The UK festival.

The event is the brainchild of Ian Bone, a founder member of Class War, whose past activities do little to inspire trust among old hands at anarchist politics. At one point Bone left the Class War Federation to set up the rival Class War Organisation, which collapsed after a single issue of its national newspaper. Among revolutionary anarchists Anarchy In The UK is derisively referred to as The Bone Show. While the festival will thrill all rebellious punk squatters, the major British anarchist groups are refusing to participate in what they perceive as a desperate attempt to revive the careers of some second-rate rock bands.

An obsession with autonomy, or freedom, is what characterises all anarchist thought. Naturally, this leads to a great deal of sectarianism. One of the major divisions within anarchist thinking is between collectivist and individualist ideologies. While anarcho-individualists have never attempted to build mass political organisations, their collectivist brethren find that although there is a great deal of support for anarchist ideas, very few people are willing to become paid up members of the movement. Indeed, no British anarchist group has an active membership of more than a hundred individuals.

When the tabloid press report that Class War are responsible for the riots that have broken out during recent demonstrations, this is patently absurd. Street violence of this type is the result of the utter frustration many people feel at the huge increase in poverty that has accompanied the dismantling of the welfare state. Class War are not in a position to organise riots – almost all their time and energy is put into producing and selling their newspaper. Most of the Class War groups around the country consist of one or two individuals with a post box address and a can of spray paint. While a percentage of the people participating in riots may have become sympathetic towards anarchist ideas after experiencing unemployment and heavy handed policing, very few of them are members of any political organisation.

Easily the most active strand of British anarchism throughout the eighties was that of pacifism and non-violence. Many anarchists who are happy to glue the locks of butchers and participate in animal rights campaigns, wouldn't dream of taking part in a riot. Likewise, anarcho-individualists and anarcho-capitalists are generally contemptuous of demonstrations and acts of public disorder. Many of the younger and more committed class struggle anarchists who do view rioting as a viable political tactic, quickly leave the movement. They often find themselves unable to resist the lure of left-communist splinter groups. In attacking democracy as a bourgeois distraction, organisations such as the International Communist Current provide an ideology which is much more coherent than that of the anarchist movement.

One of the attractions of anarchism is that it can be practised as a life-style that doesn't require a great deal of commitment. Bohemian types may voice support for Class War, but they are unlikely to join the group because that would entail standing on street corners selling political literature and attending boring meetings. Likewise, squatters may find the doctrine of anarcho-syndicalism appealing, without actually wanting to go into some industrial workplace to participate in rank and file activism.

Class War began as a witty attack on both the left and anarcho-pacifism. Today it is a poor man's SWP, as obsessed as the next revolutionary splinter group with selling the paper and building the party. In a mirror image of this process, Ian Bone has reverted to the type of anarchism that was once reviled in the pages of Class War. CND, pacifists and scruffy punks used to be the subject of Bone's invective, now he is actively promoting their interests with the Anarchy In The UK festival. This includes concerts by The Levellers and Conflict, alongside workshops on such stimulating topics as Love, and Liberating Our Meetings.

First published in *The Independent,* 25 October 1994

THE PALINGENESIS OF THE AVANT-GARDE

ONE OF THE PROBLEMS with recent academic critiques of the avant-garde is the way in which 'anti-art' has been conceptualised as privileging space over time. As a consequence, there has been little interest in viewing the avant-garde teleologically. Peter Burger in *Theory Of The Avant-Garde* (University of Minnesota, Minneapolis 1984) tends to interpret the avant-garde through the prism of Dada and Surrealism. A correction to this tendency begins to emerge in works such as Andrew Hewitt's *Fascist Modernism: Aesthetics, Politics, And The Avant-Garde* (Stanford University Press, California 1993), a work that focuses on Futurism. However, while this move 'backwards' in 'time' is most welcome, academic theorising about the avant-garde has yet to get to grips with post-war phenomena such as Lettrism and Situationism.

What can most usefully be lifted from Burger is the notion of the avant-garde as an attack on the institution of art, which emerges in opposition to the absurd assumption that Dada and Surrealism were merely an attempt to supersede the dominant artistic styles of their epoch. With regard to the author of *Theory Of The Avant-Garde* and his collaborator in criticism Christa Burger, Hewitt problematises the idea of the autonomy of art that they took up from the Frankfurt School. The following passage from *Fascist Modernism* (page 59) is typical of Hewitt's polemic:

> If capitalism provides the material preconditions for autonomous art, then it is the philosophical tradition of German Idealism that provides its ideological legitimation. At the end of

the eighteenth century the emerging literature is assigned a place within a discursive hierarchy regulated by the philosophy of Idealism. Thus, while art might be said to resist at the level of content capitalism's tendency toward economic rationalization, it can do so only within a prerationalized set of philosophical relationships. Contrary to its ideological status in the nineteenth century as an escape from ubiquitous social forces of rationalization, autonomous art is also a product of those forces.

It has long been a banality among 'radical economists' that choice within the 'free market system' is already and always ideological; that rather than being 'value free,' choice (which is inevitably preconditioned) is an arbitrary *a priori* value. The 'free market' has never existed, it is a utopian construct designed to mask the 'social' forces that actually shape the economy. Historically, as 'the arts' are liberated from the shackles of the patronage system and thereby become 'Art' in its modern sense, precisely at that moment when the commodification of culture brings about the possibility of its ideological 'autonomy,' the institution of art emerges to regulate the cultural field. It follows from this that in attacking the institution of art, the avant-garde ought to develop a critique of commodity relations. The failure of the classical avant-garde, and I would subsume the Situationist International within this category, is its failure to make this leap to an issue that lies at the heart of Marxist economics. This failure arises from a desire on the part of the classical avant-garde to integrate art and life. The classical avant-garde is utopian precisely because it wants to deregulate art; but this literal/metaphorical acceptance of the absurd claims made by Capital's ideological apologists (who necessarily propagate theories which imply that art does, or at least can, exist in the 'beyond' as a secular religion that 'transcends' commodity relations) is not without certain merits, because ultimately it brings those operating within the institution of art into conflict with the very forces that legitimate 'artistic' activity.

It is within the parameters of such a discourse that we must situate the 'praxis' of the Situationist International. Guy Debord states in *Thesis 191* of *Society Of Spectacle* (Black & Red, Detroit 1970, revised 1977) that:

> Dadaism and Surrealism are the two currents which mark the end of modern art. They are contemporaries, though only in a relatively conscious matter, of the last great assault of the revolutionary proletarian movement; and the defeat of this movement, which left them imprisoned in the same artistic field whose decrepitude they had announced, is the basic reason for their immobilization. Dadaism and Surrealism are at once historically related and opposed to each other. This opposition, which each of them considered to be its most important and radical contribution, reveals the internal inadequacy of their critique, which each developed one-sidedly. Dadaism wanted to suppress art without realizing it; Surrealism wanted to realize art without suppressing it. The critical position later elaborated by the Situationists has shown that the suppression and the realization of art are inseparable aspects of a single supersession of art.

Debord, whose 'anti-career' began with a full-length feature film *Howlings In Favour Of De Sade* which contained no images, just black film stock interspersed with bursts of white light, was incapable of stepping outside the frame of reference provided by the institution of art, and instead theorised his way back to a one-sided understanding of Hegel. It is perfectly clear from both *The Philosophical Propaedeutic (The Science of the Concept, Third Section, The Pure Exhibition of Spirit, Theses 203-207)* and the *Philosophy Of Mind: Being Part Three of the Encyclopaedia of the Philosophical Sciences (Section Three – Absolute Mind, Theses 553-571)* that within the Hegelian system the supersession of art is in fact found in revealed religion.

Since, among the more advanced sections of the 'bourgeoisie,' 'art' had by Debord's day come to replace revealed religion, the Situationists were forced to skip this particular Hegelian inversion, and instead jump forward to philosophy which represents the highest achievement of 'absolute mind' in Hegel's system. In line with the young Marx, Debord viewed the proletariat as the subject that would realise philosophy. The Situationist conception of the supersession of art is also filtered through the ideas of August von Cieszkowski, whose 1838 tome *Prolegomena zur Historiosophie* was dedicated to the notion that "the deed and social activity will now overcome (supersede) philosophy." It was this source that provided the Situationists with the material to complete their false 'sublation,' allowing them to arrive back at the final category of romantic art within the Hegelian system, that is to say poetry.

Raoul Vaneigem states in *The Revolution Of Everyday Life* (Rebel Press and Left Bank Books, London and Seattle 1983, page 153) that: "Poetry is.... 'making,' but 'making' restored to the purity of its moment of genesis – seen, in other words, from the point of view of the totality." In the sixties, Debord and Vaneigem claimed that they'd superseded the avant-garde and were consequently 'making' a 'revolutionary' situation that went beyond the point of no return. However, all the Situationists actually succeeded in doing was restating the failures of Dada and Surrealism in Hegelian terminology, with the inevitable consequence that their critique was in many ways much less 'advanced' than that of their 'precursors'. Debord, who was a better theorist than his 'comrade' Vaneigem, appeared to be aware of this slippage although he didn't know how to 'overcome' it, and the fragment of Cieszkowski cited in the celluloid version of *Society Of The Spectacle* (an English translation of the script can be found in *Society Of The Spectacle And Other Films,* Rebel Press, London 1992, page 71) is most telling: "Therefore, after the direct practice of art has ceased to be the most distinguished thing, and this predicate has been devolved onto theory, such as it is, it detaches itself presently from the latter, in so far as a synthetic post-theoretical practice is formed, which has as its primary goal to be the foundation and the truth of art as philosophy."

Hewitt states in *Fascist Modernism* (page 85) that: "History, to the artists of the avant-garde, is available as commodity; and the commodity, in turn, is intrinsically 'historical,' second-hand. Perhaps, after all, the avant-garde *does* develop a style, one of *bricolage*, in which the commodification of history and the historicization of the commodity (that is, aestheticization and politicization respectively) converge." I agree with Peter Burger when he suggests, in *Theory Of The Avant-Garde,* that the failure of the Dadaist and Surrealist assault on the institution of art led to a widening of the definition of what is acceptable as art. This was a double-edged 'failure,' arising as it did from the desire of the classical avant-garde to integrate 'art' and life, because as Hewitt implies, it leads to the history of art becoming available to the artist as a commodity. However, since the ideological 'autonomy' of art is grounded in its status as a commodity with a market value regulated by the institution of art, it must inevitably be protected as a piece of 'intellectual property' against its free use as a piece of *bricolage* in later works of art.

It comes as no surprise that as early as 1959, the Situationist Guy Debord had to rework his film *On The Passage Of A Few Persons Through A Rather Brief Period Of Time* because he was unable to buy the rights to many of the scenes he wished to re-use from Hollywood 'classics.' Debord's constant recourse to cliché is undoubtedly self-conscious and iconoclastic, so perhaps it is not ironic that his 'wholly new type of film' should sit very easily within one of the most despised cinematic genres of the post-war period, that of the mondo movie. Nevertheless, Debord was much more than simply a plagiarist, when his output is viewed from the perspective of avant-garde film-making, it appears highly innovative.

Once the practice of appropriation became widespread within the field of art, that is to say within that field of cultural practices regulated by the institution of art, then art as a discourse had reached its historical limits. These contradictions cannot be resolved within the discourse of art; within this discursive field it is not possible to advance beyond the solution offered by Hegel for whom "plagiarism would have to be a matter of honour and held in check by honour" (*Philosophy Of Right, Thesis 69*). In other words, while copyright laws remain in force, appropriation as an 'artistic' practice will continue to be dealt with by the legal system on a case by case basis. From my perspective, all that remains to be done is for the contemporary avant-garde to broaden its intransigent critique of the institution of art, while simultaneously offering a lead to all those who would step outside art as a frame of reference. This is not so much a case of 'overcoming' art as abandoning it; such a strategy was implicit in the activities of Henry Flynt, an individual active on the fringes of Fluxus who as long ago as 1962 gave up art in favour of a subjective modality which he'd named 'brend.'

The avant-garde is viewed as a nuisance by those who are happy with the world as it is. Art is a secular religion that provides a 'universal' justification for social stratification. It furnishes the ruling class with the social glue of a common culture, while simultaneously excluding the vast mass of men and wimmin from participation in this 'higher' realm. The work of art is never a simple entity, a 'thing in itself,' but is literally produced by those sets of social and institutional relationships that simultaneously legitimate it. While the contemporary avant-garde shares its precursor's desire to attack the institution of art, it also differs fundamentally from its classical predecessor. If Futurism, Dada and Surrealism wanted to integrate art and life, today's avant-garde wants to consign the former category to oblivion. This is the return at a higher level of Islamic-cum-Protestant iconoclasm. While the classical avant-garde was ultimately Deist in its attitude towards art, its progeny has taken up a stance of intransigent atheism in its antagonistic relationship to the dominant culture.

The institution of art long ago adopted the ironic pose of post-modernism, which is why the contemporary avant-garde denigrates space in favour of time. To be avant-garde is to be ahead of the pack, and this inevitably entails a 'teleological' conception of history. The avant-garde uses the 'myth of progress' in a manner analogous to Georges Sorel's conception of the 'General Strike'. The avant-garde does not believe in 'absolute' progress. Progress is simply a means of organising the present, it is a 'heuristic' device. In its 'affirmative' guises, 'progress' is an empty conception that offers men and wimmin the illusory compensation of future revenge for the humiliations they suffer in daily life. A mythic conception of progress moves wo/men to action, it is the means by which they can organise the transformation of geographical 'space'. This transformation will entail a complete break with the ideological trappings that have been familiar to us since the enlightenment. Just as the Christian religion ceased to be a viable vehicle for social contestation in the eighteenth-century, the political party as an engine of social change is now utterly exhausted. The future of mass struggle lies in what were until very recently viewed as 'fringe' phenomena, that is to say new social movements with an absurdly faked antiquity; the ever growing band of 'Druid' Councils offer an excellent example of this type of organisation.

My mythic notion of progress would be an anathema to the classical avant-gardists of the Situationist International. However, while I agree with Kant that 'culture' must be brought before the judgement of tradition, the founding father of transcendental idealism failed to ask by what tradition is any particular theory or cultural artefact to be judged? The contemporary avant-garde insists that the only tradition by which anything can be judged is one that does not yet exist, in other words, the culture we are elaborating in our theory and practice. Fluxus was not a 'genuine' avant-garde, it was simply a womb out of which intransigents capable of superseding the Situationist International have subsequently emerged. If various young adults are currently experimenting with Fluxus-style assemblages, multiples and mailings, this is a perfectly healthy first step towards avant-garde iconoclasm. To borrow Wittgenstein's metaphor, Fluxus is a ladder with which youth can climb above the world as it is, and then proceed to throw Fluxus away.

While Debord and his comrades wanted to supersede art with the 'highest' achievements of 'absolute mind,' that is to say philosophy, recent theorising about the avant-garde can be read as an attempt to transform culture into a religion of the most 'primitive' type, that of the 'divine King' or a vegetation cult. Paul Mann in *The Theory-Death Of The Avant-Garde* (Indiana University Press, Bloomington and Indianapolis 1991) states that:

> Death is necessary so that everything can be repeated and the obituary is a way to deny that death ever occurred. Under the cover of the obituary artists and critics continue exactly as before, endlessly recuperating differential forms, endlessly manufacturing shabbier and shabbier critical goods... The death of the avant-garde is old news, already finished, no longer worth discussing; but those who think so have not yet even begun to think it. There is no post: everything that claims to be so blindly repeats what it thinks it has left behind. Only those willing to remain in the death of the avant-garde, those who cease trying to drown out death's silence with the noise of neocritical production, will ever have a hope of hearing what that death articulates.

The task of the avant-garde then, is to carry on as before by providing those still trapped within the old modes of discourse with a myth that will deconstruct itself. What is as yet particular must become general, that is to say we require the social construction of a new 'subjectivity' so that, once belief is recognised as 'our' enemy, it becomes possible for 'everybody' to step outside the frames of reference provided by art, religion and philosophy. This must necessarily take the form of what the discredited 'culture' views as a fraud and a sham. Rather than attempting to 'resolve' contradictions, the 'avant-garde' puts them to 'work' as the engine of an as yet unknown 'disorder.'

Previously published in *The Hacienda Must Be Built: On the legacy of Situationist revolt, essays and documents relating to an international conference on the Situationist International, The Hacienda, Manchester 1996* (Aura, Huddersfield 1996)

THE BEAUTY OF POLLUTION: A NIGHT OUT WITH NOCTURNAL EMISSIONS

HAVING WORKED under the name Nocturnal Emissions for fifteen years, Nigel Ayers has carved out a unique reputation on the experimental music scene. His name has been dropped by everyone from Björk to Tricky. Ripped off by many but equalled by none, the fact that it is virtually impossible to obtain Nocturnal Emissions releases in record shops only adds to the cult status enjoyed by Ayers. Back in the eighties when other industrial acts were working references to Charles Manson and the Moors Murders into their repertoire, Nocturnal Emissions used suitably treated tapes of revolutionary speeches on their uncompromising albums. When Ayers relocated to Cornwall five years ago he stopped performing in public. When I heard Nocturnal Emissions were doing a one-off show I leapt at the chance to see a band I'd not seen live for nearly a decade.

Somehow it didn't surprise me that those wanting to witness this rare Nocturnal Emissions live action were instructed to go to Bromley-By-Bow tube station, from where they'd be redirected to the concert. A girl in a Beast of Bodmin Moor sweatshirt told me to make my way under the Blackwall Tunnel Northern Approach Road. The gig was scheduled to take place in a squatted flat on a derelict council estate. The Queen Victoria pub had closed up since I was last there. The thirties blocks were rotting away with broken and boarded up windows, decay proceeding apace. Given the roar and fumes from the snarled up traffic that was crawling past the estate, it had been doomed since the present six lane feeder system was constructed way back in the sixties. I took in the graffiti as I waded through broken glass. "HANG BLAIR." "LARRY IS A CHILD MOLESTER." "BOYCOTT CULTURE." It was an appropriate setting for Ayers to promote his two most recent releases, *The Beauty Of Pollution* and *Sunspot Activity*.

After I'd flashed a ticket, a bloke wearing a *Glossalalia* T-shirt ushered me into a ground floor flat. There were fifty or sixty people standing around waiting for something to happen. The water had been cut off two years before and you had to go outside if you wanted to piss. Familiar faces swam into view like so many nightmares. Bruce Gilbert, Robin 'Scanner' Rimbaud, Christoph from Praxis, most of Zion Train, Jake Black, Paul Smith, Susan Stenger, Bill Drummond. Someone handed me a bottle of Kingfisher. There wasn't a lot of light – the electricity for the PA came from a mobile generator parked outside the flat with wires looped in through the windows. When I arrived a tape of one minute Coca Cola commercials from the late sixties was blasting out. The artists featured on these corporate cuts included the likes of the Supremes, Ray Charles, Marvin Gaye, the Box Tops, Gladys Knight And The Pips, Aretha Franklin, The Moody Blues, Roy Orbison, The Troggs and least likely of all, Vanilla Fudge.

Eventually these jingles were replaced by the jarring sounds of power electronics. Slides of Princess Di flashed across a screen. Not long after this a couple beside me were swapping jokes, all of which I'd heard before. "What do Diana and Pink Floyd have in common. They both had a hit with The Wall." Standing solemnly over his keyboards Ayers announced: "The Diana funeral was a sad psychedelic remix of state propaganda and Reclaim The Streets strategies. Major roads temporarily pedestrianised and festooned with flowers. Pop music pumped out from Westminster Abbey. The M1 motorway brought to standstill from London to Northampton. However, it needs to be emphasised that car culture was celebrated in the iconography of the Diana death crash. The Mercedes was Diana's means of escape from the evil eye of the paparazzi. The patent contradictions of her public image made her seem a bit more 'human' than the rest of the Windsor gang. Unfortunately, she never gave up her designated role in perpetrating the class system..."

The couple beside me remained studiously unimpressed and continued swapping jokes. "What's the difference between a Lada and a Mercedes? Di wouldn't be seen dead in a Lada." The persistence of this banter left me with the impression that humour was the only way in which this pair could deal with being confronted by something they felt was taboo. Ayers has an ability to touch raw nerves. The harsh commentary wasn't sung and the way in which it was electronically treated made it hard to follow at times, fortunately the audience had been supplied with xeroxed transcripts. "Bickering among members of the ruling class is a means of consolidating their power. This is the trick black magicians use to conceal the obvious, to maintain the illusion of power. A chattering circle is created to distract attention away from the fact that wealth is created by the workers and then appropriated by bosses..."

While Ayers proceeded with this meditation on the capitalist social system, the performance artist John Fare was led blindfolded onto the stage. Fare cuts an eccentric figure – he wears trousers made from zips and has a diagram of a brain tattooed onto his shaven scalp. The performance artist placed his left hand on a chopping board with the fingers spread. Fare's assistant Jill Orr is partially sighted and she slammed an axe between her boyfriend's pinkies with increasing speed. Eventually the axe severed Fare's little finger. This was the end of the performance art element within the evening's entertainment. Fare was rushed across the road to St. Andrews hospital where a doctor dealt with his wound. By this time Nocturnal Emissions had finished with Diana and Ayers was performing a new piece entitled *Futurist Antiquarianism*. The audience was too shocked to take it in. People began to drift away. They'd had enough live action for one night. Ayers was happy enough at this turn of events – his reputation for alienating admirers and emptying concert halls had been convincingly preserved.

The Beauty Of Pollution and *Sunspot Activity* are available at £12 per CD from Earthly Delights, PO Box 2, Lostwithiel, Cornwall, PL22 0YY. Make cheques payable to Nigel Ayers. Send an SAE for a full catalogue of Nocturnal Emissions material.

First published in *D>Tour*, December 1997

ROYAL WATCH:
BEHIND THE LODGE DOOR

IN MY LAST COLUMN, I revealed the problems Canary Wharf Tower had created for the royal family because it is soaking up the ancient earth energies from a ley line they'd been tapping into during their black magick rituals. Since the Queen's plot to have the building blown up in a fake 'IRA' bomb outrage was foiled by the Knights of St Thomas, her eldest son has come up with a new plan for tapping into the earth energies that are an essential ingredient of royal power. Charles is secretly campaigning to have a church built inside the pyramid that caps the top of the tower. The ancient energies generated by the ley line on which the building was constructed are concentrated in this pyramid before being thrown out into space. By holding black masses in the pyramid, the prince believes he will accumulate fantastic powers.

Leading anglican clergy have been enlisted to float the plan for a church at the top of the tower. In a recent public lecture given at the Dockers Club, Richard Chartres – the new Bishop of Stepney – discussed plans to rationalise the use of church properties in the East End. Among other things, he said that churches which are no longer needed should be demolished rather than converted to other uses or left to decay. The Bishop explained that abandoned churches symbolise the increasing secularisation of society. Rather conveniently, a policy of destroying unwanted ecclesiastical properties would enable the royals to make alterations to the flow of earth energies along various ley lines. Chartres also announced a plan to build a church on a barge so that it could be moved around as it was needed. Again, this would make the channelling of ancient energies a more flexible operation. Finally, the Bishop revealed his belief that a church should be built in the pyramid that caps the Canary Wharf Tower!

Until these plans are realised, Prince Charles is temporarily using the library of Sion College as a London venue for occult activities. The college is situated near Blackfriars Bridge, on the corner of Embankment and John Carpenter Street. The premises are shared with the City Livery Club, making it an important centre of ruling class activity. It's unclear whether Geoffrey Brown, president of the college, knows what Charlie gets up to in the library. However, the Rev. Dr Thomas White, who founded Sion College, is notorious among conspiracy theorists as both a mason and a black magician. Among other indications of lodge activity still evident in the library are three masonic chairs. The seat used by the Prince of Wales bears the name Athelstan, a particularly cruel saxon king who ruled from 925 to 940. The chairs that flank this throne are both inscribed with the number 19, a reference to an occult system of dividing the year into 19 months of 19 days with four days left over for solstice and equinox celebrations.

While Charles caused something of a stir among ordinary masons when he refused to join the United Grand Lodge, he is now the head of an organisation that broke away from the notorious P2 lodge and subsequently set up its own 'Greek rite'. Major ceremonials of this irregular lodge entail young boys being sodomised and disemboweled. These rituals rarely take place in London because disposal of the bodies can be problematic in an urban area. However, such murders are an essential part of the prince's occult programme and generally take place in remote parts of the world. A double regularly replaces Charlie at public events, so that he is free to participate in black magic rituals without arousing any suspicions about his evil exploits among the British population. Parents of boys aged between eight and fourteen should keep them under close supervision in the week leading up to the summer solstice. Failure to do so could result in their abduction and murder as a part of the prince's occult activities.

First published in *Underground 2*, Summer 1993

HUNGRY IN THE FOOD HALL
STARING AT THE SALMON

An interview with the Art Attacks.

I MET STEVE SPEAR AND EDWIN POUNCEY, formerly of the Art Attacks, at Waterloo station on 25 June 1996. Bassist Marion Fudger had various work commitments and couldn't make it. We didn't know how to contact drummer John Haney, who may well be living in America. Although Steve and Marion had kept in touch, Edwin hadn't seen either of them for fourteen years. I suggested we make our way down to Lower Marsh Street, since I liked one of the pubs on that street. Edwin and Steve thought I'd led them to Streets as a joke. Actually, I hadn't been in the place for a couple of years, and I'd forgotten what it was called.

Edwin: We got together because there was a talent night at the Royal College Of Art.

Steve: I had the idea of starting a punk band. A mate said you should get Edwin from graphics to be the singer. I hadn't met Edwin before, I just went up and asked him if he wanted to be the singer in a punk band to do the talent night. I had a place to rehearse, we just cobbled something together. We had Ricky Slaughter, who later played in the Motors, as the drummer. Rob Smith from the Snakes played bass. I don't remember the name of the other guitarist. He knew a Beach Boys number, so we did that. Me and Edwin made up two songs. We were just going to do covers but someone said punk is about doing it yourself, so we decided to write some songs of our own. Edwin had one called *Subway Train* which just got faster and faster, until it exploded at the end. The other was *Rat City*. The gig went quite well. At one point I jumped off the stage and had a fight with some bloke in the audience. Someone else came up to us afterwards and asked if we wanted a gig at Wimbledon College Of Art. We said yeah. Then we had to put a set together. Edwin came over to my place and we wrote ten songs. The next gig was The Man In The Moon in the Kings Road. A guy called Paul said he wanted to be our manager, he got us more gigs, it snowballed from there.

Stewart: So when did Marion Fudger join?

Steve: After two or three gigs Rob Smith said he couldn't do it anymore. I already knew Marion from the Stockwell squatting scene, so I asked her if she wanted to play bass. She was a bit embarrassed – she went out under the name of M.S. so that no one knew it was her. Marion wanted to be a serious musician. She later taught at the Deptford Academy of Music, a kind of fame school for kids.

Stewart: After Marion joined you recorded your first and only demos.

Steve: We went into Pathway Studios in Stoke Newington and recorded *Rat City* and *Chickens In Funland*. Edwin and I paid for it. We had Robert Gotobed for that, he was just learning to be a drummer, this was before he joined Wire.

Edwin: We were interested in making up these little stories. *Rat City* was about a middle-aged guy on a treadmill. There was a lot of poetry in the songs, stuff that nobody else bothered to say in a punk band. *Chickens In Funland* was on the front of *The Sun*. It was about this traffic in chickens, where they were stuffed into arcades to play the piano or something.

Steve: It was about animal cruelty. It was a gambling thing, where you won if the chicken hit a certain key on the piano.

Stewart: You did the demos, then you got a deal with Albatross, an independent label.

Edwin: Albatross was run from the basement of Kensington Market – they had this scummy record shack selling bruised copies of Stooges albums. The guys who owned it decided to start a record label. They went looking for mugs and found us. We were the only ones they bothered with. We did *I Am A Dalek* and *Neutron Bomb* as the two sides of the single. *Dalek* is about a job I had in a department store when I left school. The general manager called me into his office and told me I was going to be a dalek in the toy department.

Stewart: It doesn't sound like relations with Albatross were particularly cordial.

Edwin: The people at Albatross were this hippie guy and his girlfriend, who was a Gypsy Rose Lee lookalike, and this other guy who always wore a suit. The guy with the suit used to come up with these really stupid ideas, like they were going to advertise our single on all the buses in London.

Steve: The hippie guy's girlfriend was a professional stripper. She just suddenly appeared on stage at the Marquee. Marion used to work for *Spare Rib* and was particularly offended.

Edwin: We were in the middle of this number and I felt this stinging on the back of my neck. I thought bloody hell, is there a wasp in here? I turned round and there was this half naked old woman whipping me. I told her to fuck off.

Steve: Me and Marion just looked at each other across the stage. There was a photo of it in *Sounds*. We were getting in the music papers all the time. Marion knew about it. She said to us they're desperate to fill up the space, so if we send in a good photo they'll use it. Underneath they'd put the dates of any gigs we had coming up. It was astonishing how easy it was.

Stewart: What happened to Albatross?

Steve: We did a gig at the Rochester Castle in Stoke Newington and they had a distribution guy come along to see us perform. We did a bad gig, they didn't like it.

Edwin: That was the one where I crawled inside the drum kit and refused to come out for the rest of the gig.

Steve: The guy comes up to us afterwards and says, "another gig like that and you're off our label." *I Am A Dalek* sold seven and a half thousand copies, it was the only record Albatross put out.

Edwin: I used to get in such a state of fright, I had to get tanked out of my brain to get on stage. In Hammersmith I handed the mike to a tramp who lumbered on stage as I wandered off. The new vocalist was this derelict screaming rubbish. Like the stalwart soldiers that they were, the rest of the band carried on.

Stewart: How did you come to have a track on the *Streets* compilation?

Steve: As a result of Paul our manager knowing the Lurkers, they were on Beggars Banquet who put it out. The label paid for us to go into a flash studio to record *Arabs In 'Arrads,* which our drummer John Haney wrote the words for. We went on a tour as a result of that. We did places like Nikkers in Keighley.

Edwin: We went all over the place to promote that *Streets* album, mostly Yorkshire.

Steve: It was a weird tour because you'd get a good sized crowd but the venues were always these northern soul clubs. The stages were on half floors. You'd do the gig and everyone would be looking down at you, watching from the gallery where the bar was. You'd be going crazy and the crowd didn't react at all. They'd just stand there and stare.

Edwin: It was a Mecca dance hall type set-up. The audience would be leaning on balconies, looking at us going mad. They'd be going to their girlfriends, do you fancy another babycham? Before I went on at one of these places I had a fight with a Bert Weedon fan. This bloke says, "you're one of them punks aren't ya." I said, "I'm in one of these bands playing tonight." I'd had a few and I was getting revved up. The bloke asked me what I thought of Bert Weedon. I said, "to be honest I think he's an absolute cunt." This bloke goes, "I'll have you know I adore Bert Weedon!" Then he whacked me in the mouth. This is a minute before we go on and my mouth is bleeding badly. The audience went a bit mad, like they'd scented blood. I just said, "a Bert Weedon fan did this to me."

Stewart: Apart from the *Streets* tour, did you play out of London much?

Steve: We did gigs with Generation X, they weren't our favourite band. Their audience was young kids, so it was difficult to deal with them. These kids were really into it. We used to take the piss out of Billy Idol just to warm the audience up. We did loads of gigs with Generation X, until we said we wouldn't do any more because we didn't think they were very good for us.

Edwin: It all culminated in their stupid road crew turning the mikes off when we were playing in Croydon. There's this hall full of spitting kids, we're just standing on stage and there's no sound coming out. We were out there and we could see the road crew laughing at the back. We got gobbed on beyond belief, we were just dripping.

Steve: You always got gobbed on with Billy Idol, his crowd were really into spitting. We did all over with Generation X. Marquee, Colchester, Brunel Rooms in Swindon. We did a lot of gigs with 999, a lot with the Lurkers, quite a few with the Motors coz I knew them. We also did art college gigs and any other gigs we could pick up. We did most of the London pubs during the eighteen months we were together. We had Bill Oddie in the audience at the Rat Club in Kings Cross. There were all these women in the audience complaining it was too loud. The band on before us was the remains of Thunderclap Newman. We go on and half the crowd leave during our set. Then the management wouldn't pay us, so we had to have a huge argument to get half our money.

Stewart: Did you ever get approached by major labels?

Steve: We were quite antagonistic towards big record companies. We really wanted to be small and do our own thing, but we didn't have the money we needed to make the band work properly.

Stewart: Did the band ever make money?

Steve: The gigs broke even. We'd do a support at the Marquee with the Motors and they'd pay us a fiver. It was fuck all. Later, it went up to a tenner. Student Unions always paid more, they were a good gig. We did Rock Against Racism gigs because they paid good money. They paid full expenses, to us that was a lot of money. Rock Against Racism paid fifty quid for a gig.

Stewart: You must have ended up out of pocket.

Steve: We never saw any financial return for the time we put in. The manager never took any money either. Maybe he had a few drinks out of our gig expenses. We spent a lot of time rehearsing.

Edwin: We used to write one or two songs a week. We must have had fifty songs. If we'd had the money, I'd have probably made a real go of it. A lot of the songs were never recorded.

Stewart: Did you get paid for your records?

Steve: We got some money from the Tagmemics seven inch, which was a post-Art Attacks project, because the guy who put it out in America sent a bunch of records over. Edwin took those round and sold them through places like Rough Trade. We kept the money we got from that. I once got a juke box plays royalty cheque for six pounds eighty-four. We've had our MCPS royalties.

Edwin: Because John Peel used to play *I Am A Dalek*.

Steve: I got about three hundred pounds out of the Art Attacks over the years, that's everything that ever came in.

Stewart: How did the tracks *Animal Bondage* and *Frankenstein's Heartbeat* end up on the *Live At The Vortex* album?

Steve: We used to play the Vortex all the time. It was weird, we'd insult the management from the stage but they always wanted us back. The Vortex was a good gig because it used to get crowded.

Edwin: We played with Squeeze once at the Marquee, can you imagine that? We were top of the bill!

Steve: They always used to overload the Marquee in the old days, people would be falling over the front of the stage.

Stewart: The Marquee had such a great history, with bands like The Who paying their dues there.

Steve: Keith Moon came into the dressing room when we played the Nashville. He was trying to hype us up before we went on stage.

Edwin: I had a headache and dissed Keith Moon. I felt bad about it afterwards. He was trying to be nice, but I dissed him. He was a great guy Keith Moon, but he arrived at a bad time. I was just preparing to go on, and the last thing I wanted was some guy telling me what to do. I was trying to focus all my energy to go out there and do it. It was serious shit, it was like going to war.

Stewart: Why did the band break up?

Edwin: What finished it for me was the worry about not getting my degree. I really wanted to get that degree. I had to prove I could do it, so everything else had to go. Fresh put out a posthumous first and last release, *Punk Rock Stars* backed with *Rat City*. Later on, after the Art Attacks, we went into Pathway as the Tagmemics and recorded three new songs, *Chimneys, (Do The) Big Baby* and *Take Your Brain Out For A Walk*. It was an experiment, we never did any more gigs but the tracks were issued by Index. The songs are very surreal and indicate the way the Art Attacks would have developed if we'd stayed together. Devo used to include a cover of *Take Your Brain Out For A Walk* in their live set.

Steve: At that time, we were getting fed up with the whole scene, it was crass and commercial. I started out with the idea that the punk scene would shake up the music industry. I wanted to see thousands of people releasing their own records. Just whacking them out and selling them at gigs. I felt that was getting eaten up.

First published in the booklet accompanying the CD
Outrage & Horror by the Art Attacks
(Overground, Newcastle and Hove 1996)

FROM PORN TO ART

MANET'S *OLYMPIA* was painted in 1863 and images of sexual exploitation have been popular among artists ever since. Although art has long provided bashful blokes with illicit kicks under the guise of 'self-improvement', it is only more recently that porn stars began making the transition from the video underground to the cultural mainstream. Nevertheless, sustaining a straight movie career can be difficult. Teenage porn sensation Traci Lords was elevated to matinee status thanks to a lead role in *Cry Baby*, but currently makes techno records after several box-office flops.

Pornography is an integral part of the entertainment business, and the vehicles created for its stars are every bit as formulaic as Hollywood blockbusters. While there may be less money in more experimental areas like performance art, such genres offer a freedom that is attractive to individuals who are sick of being type-cast. Porn veteran Annie Sprinkle is typical of those who want to escape the limitations imposed on them by mass culture: "The reason I got out of porn and moved into art is because there's more room for experimentation in art. I can be myself."

Gay porn stars are making this transition too. Aiden Shaw whose autobiography *Brutal* was published last year, has been pulling in punters at prestigious venues such as the Institute Of Contemporary Arts. Shaw's act, which lies somewhere between performance art and Chippendale-style pop, has been packaged as part of a musical review that also features cult rockers Minty. While cynics see these gallery escapades as a neat way of marketing over-exposed sex stars to a fresh audience, a trooper like Annie Sprinkle radiates sincerity as she hard sells 'post porn modernism' as a 'new age sexuality': "Sex is a path to enlightenment. Women producing porn will push things in a positive direction."

One woman who relishes breaking down sexual boundaries is Cosey Fanni Tutti, born Christine Carol Newby in 1951. Between 1974 and 1976 Tutti worked as a glamour model for *Fiesta, Curious* and *Ladybirds,* then exhibited her centre-spreads in art galleries. Tutti also toured London pubs as a stripper, as well as appearing in films such as *Confessions Of A Superstud* and *I'm Not Feeling Myself Tonight,* all in the name of art. These activities are currently being researched by Simon Ford, a post-graduate student at the Courtauld Institute of Art.

"The strength of Tutti's work lies in its play on artistic authenticity," Ford explains. "For this to register there had to be a certain loss of agency in the studio stages of its production. It was the ability to draw on real experiences as a real model in the fantasy world of pornography that made it so hard for critics to deal with in the seventies. It is the explicit play on notions of authenticity and identity through a foregrounding of pornography as a signifying system, that marks out Tutti's work as a significant contribution to the feminist critique of an essentialised femininity."

Tutti favours plainer words when defending her activities: "You get feminists saying you're being exploited and all the rest of it. But it's not like that. It's a total power trip. When you're being exploited, it's when you're doing something you're not comfortable with. Where it's not you. Where someone is saying 'do this.' " Porn queen La Cicciolina, whose stormy relationship with Jeff Koons was recorded in a series of hardcore poses that her partner marketed as art, seems to have been more ruthlessly exploited on the gallery circuit than during her glory years in glamour. Since the breakdown of her marriage, La Cicciolina has disappeared into a post-porn wilderness.

Art and porn are mirror images of each other. Sex sells and the main thing distinguishing these two genres is the more open and honest approach of sleaze merchants. Nevertheless, even someone as pretentious as film-maker Michael Winner was able to begin his career with the nudie abomination *Some Like It Cool,* while numerous struggling actresses have made ends meet by appearing in blue movies. Elaine Page of *Evita* fame cameos in *Adventures Of A Plumbers Mate,* while Joanna Lumley features in *Games That Lovers Play.* Both the art and pornographic worlds are fashion based. In each there is a constant turnover of faces. While former porn stars make adequate artists, let's hope there isn't a widespread attempt at reversing this process. I don't think I could stomach looking at Rachel Whiteread or Allen Jones with their kit off.

First published in *Variant, Vol. 2 no 6,* Autumn 1998

PUNK ROCK DRUNK IN HELSINKI

SOMETIMES I WONDER if Bill Drummond ever sleeps. I had to drag myself out of bed to answer yet another of his early morning calls. He'd phoned to tell me that we weren't going to meet at The Tea Room on Museum Street. Instead, I was to go to Heathrow Airport and catch a flight to Helsinki, a ticket was waiting for me at the Finnair desk. I was met at Helsinki airport by a young Finnish writer called Petteri Paksuniemi. Petteri took me to his flat where I was introduced to his girlfriend Sibelius, a painter and top face on the Finnish underground. Sibelius is the great granddaughter of the famous composer with whom she shares her name. Petteri opened a bottle of Four Roses, a particularly foul bourbon, while Sibelius grabbed some beers from the fridge, which we drank as chasers.

We imbibed steadily, then headed for The Old Student's House, a bar near the railway station. I drank a Lapin Kulta before asking when Bill was going to show. Petteri ignored the question, Sibelius explained that if her boyfriend had wanted to talk he'd have taken me to a coffee house. Drinking is a serious business in Finland and after these few words, Sibelius clammed up too. I was knocking back beers, while Petteri and his girlfriend were downing a peculiar cocktail of milk, vodka, coffee liqueur and ice. After a long and pregnant silence, three guys turned up who were introduced as Jape, Vassa and Sid of the Fukits, "the best fucking punk band in Finland."

While the Fukits were at the bar, Petteri interrupted his libations to explain that this was the group I'd come to Helsinki to review. I retorted that I'd travelled to Finland to meet up with Bill Drummond, and that I'd never heard of the Fukits. Petteri laughed before announcing that Bill had gone to Estonia for a few days. It transpired that the Fukits were one of several bands Drummond had signed to a Finnish indie label. I was told that Bill wanted the Fukits to release three raw seven inches and an album. After that they'd agreed to split, so that they'd be transformed into a posthumous legend. The records will be issued in limited editions of two hundred, with the first due to appear imminently. Drummond had lured me to Helsinki under false pretences; he didn't want to meet up, he wanted me to rave about the Fukits in the pages of *D>Tour*.

Several drinks later, Petteri announced that he needed to buy some porn since he was bored with the sex videos he had at home. He promised he'd be back within thirty minutes. Sibelius left too – she wanted to get on with some painting. Once the Fukits had me on my own, they grilled me about innumerable obscure English punk bands from the late seventies. Did I know if there were any unreleased studio recordings by The Users? Of course not. After an hour of this banter, Jape used a pay phone to call Petteri's mobile and a short conversation left him fuming. His friend was completely smashed after several days of serious drinking and had fallen asleep in the toilet of the Academic Bookshop. If Petteri hadn't received Jape's call, he wouldn't have woken. Jape cursed writers for their inability to stay away from books, then ranted about Petteri using porn as an excuse to sneak off and service a real vice.

Once Petteri caught up with us, we hopped a tram to the east side of Helsinki. We were going to eat at Jape's apartment. Jape's girlfriend had made a salad and Karelian pies. The food had to wait while we had an aperitif of Jack Daniel's. Petteri poured himself a generous treble and then added milk before knocking it back. Vassa was disgusted by this act and berated his friend for ruining good bourbon. We drank beers with our food. I enjoyed the traditional savoury pastries made with a potato filling, piling them high with a sauce of whipped butter and eggs. Once we'd had our fill, we finished the bottle of Jack Daniel's. After this, we trooped across the street to the Café Melba. The Fukits hadn't been booked to play – it was an open night at the club and anyone could just get up and do something. Jape greeted a few friends, while the rest of us made a beeline for the bar.

A bunch of long-hairs were murdering *California Dreaming* as I ordered a lager. Some hippies did a couple of blues numbers, then got off stage and there was a poetry recital which was ignored by the entire audience. Eventually the Fukits got their turn and after retuning their borrowed guitars, tore through several up tempo numbers. Petteri and some of his mates pogoed madly, while hippies and poets yelled abuse. The organisers asked the band to get off stage and let someone else do something. The Fukits pretended not to hear this request and launched into their anthem *Punk Rock Drunk*. "Buy me a beer, buy me two, tomorrow I won't remember you, I wanna get drunk, I wanna fuck shit up, I'm nobody's fool and I don't need you."

A hippie threw a beer glass and it shattered against Jape's borrowed guitar. Petteri grabbed hold of the guy and threw him through a plate glass window. Seconds later, the band were laying into some long-hairs who'd jumped on top of Petteri. The Fukits were out-numbered but they are hardened street fighters. Most of their opponents had fled before the sound of wailing police sirens drove the band out of the café. We headed downtown, the first port of call being Club Soda. The place was packed with pretty girls, most of whom turned down repeated requests for a pogo. We hung around drinking to an eclectic mix of dance and easy sounds before making our way to a strip joint. The boys had finally found somewhere their antics were appreciated. One stripper delighted the Fukits by getting fresh with Petteri, who was too drunk to fuck and wasn't the least bit interested in paying for sex.

First published in *D>Tour*, January 1998

THE ART OF CHAUVINISM
IN BRITAIN AND FRANCE

CONTEMPORARY ART simultaneously produces, and is produced by, the social forms it serves to legitimate. 'Western' society is in a state of crisis, therefore 'western' culture is an important theatre of operations for those who wish to intervene in this crisis. The cultural realm, always an area of major significance to the ruling class, has come to occupy an even more important hegemonic position in 'western' society since the switch to a service economy. The 'major' European nations no longer enjoy economic hegemony over the rest of the world, and the European ruling classes clearly view culture as a vehicle through which they can 'will' their way back to global dominance. With every passing day, it becomes increasingly apparent that empty rhetoric about a New World Order was the last resort of American politicians hoping to mask the economic eclipse of 'the West' by the emerging markets of South-East Asia. A few years ago, George Bush was speaking of the New World Order as if this meant that Japan had replaced Russia as the power jointly dominating the world alongside the USA. In fact, the Japanese economy is stagnating, its unwieldy corporate structure outflanked by the smaller units of capitalist production favoured in 'city states' such as Singapore.

The city-centred development of capital around the Pacific Rim is unlikely to result in a return to the patronage system of the early Renaissance. The birth of art in its modern sense dates from the breakdown of this system. Art's appearance of autonomy is derived from the commodification of objects produced speculatively and sold on the 'open' market, thereby escaping some of the ideological constraints of the pre-Renaissance patronage system but shackled all the same by social forms which produce, and are produced by, the institution of art. Despite its 'internationalist' pretensions and its development through and across various cultures, the institution of art has in practice served the interests of a narrow-minded nationalism. This observation is true of far more than simply the most obviously totalitarian forms of art such as social realism. The American intelligence service ploughed vast amounts of money into promoting abstract expressionism, as has recently been revealed in articles such as 'Modern Art Was CIA "Weapon"' (*Independent On Sunday*, 22 October 1995). As a result, New York was able to 'steal' the 'idea' of the 'avant-garde' from Paris, while simultaneously attempting to banish the more intransigent proponents of cultural materialism, who remain a spectre haunting both 'the East' and 'the West'. As far as I am concerned, Jean-Paul Sartre doesn't enter into this equation. Although the CIA may have feared Sartre's influence, his work is simply rehashed Heidegger, a fact that makes him, alongside hacks like Bertrand Russell and Karl Popper, one of the most despised philosophers of the twentieth century.

Since ancient Greece forms the founding myth of 'Europe', it is only natural that intense rivalry for the mantle of heir to the classical 'heritage' predates the formation of the modern nation state. As Jean Seznec observes in *The Survival Of The Pagan Gods: The Mythological Tradition and Its Place in Renaissance Humanism and Art* (Princetown University Press, New Jersey 1972, p. 18): "In the twelfth century, cultivated men were already aware of the Greco-Roman origins of their culture, and Chrestien de Troyes affirms the idea that France had garnered the patrimony of antique virtue and culture..." Different forms of pseudo-classicism were developed by the different cultures of 'Europe,' but those who styled themselves as 'French' proved most adept at claiming the 'heritage' that was Greece and Rome, while simultaneously inventing nationalism as we know it today.

Although it was Hegel and Marx who provided revolutionaries with the theoretical tools with which they could attempt to forge a passage to the practical goal of overthrowing the state, the wily 'French' finding themselves unable to overcome 'German' idealism, made Paris the 'spiritual' home of revolution. From 1789, via the Commune, to the events of May '68 and more recent strike waves, the militancy of both 'French' workers and the 'French' bourgeoisie has impressed 'Anglo-American' radicals. James H. Billington, who addresses this phenomena in *Fire In The Minds Of Men: Origins of the Revolutionary Faith* (Basic Books, New York 1980, p. 26), states that:

> The cafés in the arcades and the 'circus' in the center of the Palais-Royal incubated an intellectual opposition that went beyond the mild Whiggish reformism of the London coffee-houses that the House of Orléans had originally sought to imitate... If the French Revolution can be said to have begun in any single spot at any single moment, it may have been in the gardens of the Palais-Royal at about 3.30 in the afternoon of Sunday, July 12 1789, when Camille Desmoulins climbed up on a table and cried *Aux armes!* to the milling crowd... the crowd began coursing out onto the streets carrying busts of Necker and the Duke of Orléans.

Thus the 'French' transformed Paris into the centre of both the old world and a world yet to come. The classical tradition was appropriated for the 'benefit' of 'French' culture, while the 'first' modern political revolution is historicised as having been brewed in the cafés of Paris, establishments which later became the 'centre' of modern art. Therefore, it will surprise no one that early in 1996 André Bernard and others involved with the Parisian cultural bulletin *Ab Irato,* were soliciting responses to the question "will the New World Order mean a New Cultural Order?" The New World Order is a chimera, a mask to cover a crisis of confidence that has swept through the 'western' 'democracies' in the wake of their alleged victory over a rival power block. What I wish to do, is examine the ways in which this crisis has manifested itself in relation to the institution of art and, in particular, various debates generated by the utter bankruptcy of serious culture.

Before moving on to examine the phenomena of the 'young British artist', I wish to deal briefly with Barthélémy Schwarz's text 'From The Subversion Of Society By Art To The Subsidy Of Art By Society,' (*Le Monde Libertaire 4*, July/August 1995), which was distributed alongside André Bernard's call for papers responding to the question "will the New World Order mean a New Cultural Order?" In the past, Schwarz has made useful criticisms of situationist fallacies, see for example the translated review of Guy Debord's *Cette mauvais réputation* included in *Transgressions: A Journal Of Urban Explorations 1,* (University Of Newcastle 1995, p. 79-81). Therefore, it is a little disconcerting to find Schwarz claiming that "it is not possible to have the realisation of art without the suppression of capitalism." Among Hegelians, there is an ongoing debate over whether Hegel was positing the death of art through its supersession by revealed religion and ultimately philosophy within his hierarchically structured system. The SI's desire to realise and suppress art is a clear indication of how it positioned itself as an organisation within this debate. It was the inability of Debord and his friends to theorise beyond the surface phenomena of capitalist society that led them to supersede art with 'theory', in effect 'philosophy'. What we call art is a product of commodification, it does not exist in non-capitalist societies and, as a consequence, Schwarz's call for the realisation of art through social revolution beggars belief.

Schwarz's ideas are mired in French nationalism precisely because he wishes to defend art and the easiest way for him to do so given his geographical location is to adopt the tried and trusted perspectives of a Paris-centred 'revolutionary' 'avant-garde'. From the standpoint of 'art theory', Schwarz makes some clever innovations. For example, his notion of mixed-economy art, which is characterised as "the art of the period running from the Liberation... up to the crisis today... on the one hand, the sham artists of the private sector... of which the main features are accumulation, destruction, serialisation... on the other hand, the sham artists... of the State... of whom the characteristics are taxonomy, parcelling, labelling, sorting, defining, naming..." Nevertheless, by accepting the notion of the mixed economy as a phenomena peculiarly characteristic of the second half of the twentieth century and applying it to art, Schwarz is adopting the outlook of a bourgeois ideologue. The notion of a free market is completely utopian; historically capitalism has always tended towards a mixed economy, although the level of state intervention has obviously varied over time. Likewise, by using the notion of the 'Liberation' without so much as quote marks around it, Schwarz is operating from a very narrow social perspective, since as a form of historical periodisation it makes no sense to the vast majority of people in the world.

Since art has traditionally been defended on the basis of its universal validity, its apologists often find it convenient to disguise the essentially bourgeois character of the views they hold. However, as Simon Ford documents in his article *Myth Making,* (*Art Monthly 194,* March 1996), those critics cheer- leading the promotion of young British artists (yBa) feel little inclination to place constraints on their expressions of chauvinism as they cynically celebrate the existence of a phenomenon that their 'critical' activities have helped bring into being:

> The question as to whether the myth of the yBa is nationalistic
> does not exhaust itself with an examination of individual works
> but also in how the work is used and promoted abroad. By
> appealing to national pride the myth of the yBa seeks to instil
> in its audience a sense of national identity which is where myth

fades into ideology. This group has been utilised as cultural ambassadors representing and defining 'British' culture abroad... representing Britain in full 'enterprise culture' bloom.

Ironically, one of the more insidious expressions of this outburst of cultural chauvinism, *Mad For It! Bank and the New British Art* by John Roberts (*Everything 18,* London 1996), appeared more or less simultaneously with Ford's piece. Roberts attempts to theorise the yBa as a bulwark against criticisms of art made from a class perspective:

> The working-class philistine may be the excluded disaffirmative presence of art's professional self-reification, but this does not mean that working-class refusal of art's reification is the excluded truth of art. This sociological formalism is what is wrong with the post-aesthetic followers of Pierre Bourdieu who takes the truth of art to lie solely in its class exclusion... the 'philistine' is a discursive construction which shifts position depending on what constitutes 'proper' or 'correct' aesthetic behaviour... For there is the unthinking stupidity of the philistine who sees his or her rejection of the dominant discourses of modern art as univocally true, and the thinking stupidity of the philistine who sees his or her rejection of the dominant discourses of modern art as a matter of ethical positioning. The latter, in my view, underscores the work of Bank and a number of other young British artists (Gavin Turk, Gillian Wearing, Dave Beech, David Burrows).

Roberts resorts to creating a cardboard opponent and then knocking it down. To reduce art to its class exclusions is clearly absurd, since even for Bourdieu art very obviously provides the ruling class with the ideological glue of a common culture. In fact, many other critiques have been made of art, from Henry Flynt's attack upon it as the imposition of an alien subjectivity to Jean Gimpel's rationalist moral argument. Sociology, like art 'criticism', is a bourgeois specialisation which seeks to maintain separate categories of knowledge as, among other things, a buttress to the class position of academics like Roberts, who is thus able to pose as a middle-class expert on a specific form of discourse. Roberts attacks sociology for its reductive formalism, something that is a feature common to all academic specialisations including art 'criticism', precisely because he does not wish to deal with materialist critiques that do not reduce the organisation of power to a simple question of class categories, but instead allow other specificities, other patterns of exploitation and exclusion, to be seen in relation to each other and the broader articulation of power. Likewise, Roberts fails to address why, in his words, "after postmodernism the bridging of the 'great divide' between popular culture and high culture is formally a dead issue." Roberts is able to make this bald assertion by ignoring the critique of the institution of art elaborated by, among others, Roger L. Taylor in his book *Art An Enemy Of The People* (Harvester Press, Hassocks 1978), and because 'postmodernism', most especially in its yBa form, represents the triumphant re-emergence of what Igor Golomstock has described as being, after modernism, the second international style of twentieth-century culture, that is to say totalitarian art.

With the exhaustion of modernism, it became necessary for the ruling elite to revive the discourse of totalitarian art, and just as National Socialism was a brand of aesthetic politics, so 'postmodernism' is ultimately cultural fascism. The identity politics of the democratic 'left' was long ago appropriated by the New Right for the defence of 'European particularism.' Naturally, both pop art and performance were important precursors to these trends, with Beuys, Warhol and Gilbert & George being the leading exponents of this tendency as modernism entered its final phase of decline. One of the functions of totalitarian culture is to simultaneously mask and highlight the class exclusions of art by reaching out to the 'masses' and encouraging them to view certain cultural artefacts as windows into a 'higher' realm, where their inclusion as passive spectators is actually a mark of their exclusion from participation in 'serious' culture in any meaningful sense. Ford in *Myth Making* describes how the "origination and propagation of the [yBa] myth are firstly the responsibility of the contemporary arts establishment. The myth then becomes a feature of the mediation between the art world and a wider audience by the mass media."

The yBa appeals to those who have made their money from pop and fashion precisely because such people are upwardly mobile and, along with the yBa, form part of a pincher attack on Europe aimed at re-establishing Anglo-American hegemony in culture. It should go without saying that so called Brit-pop is grounded in exactly the same sixties nostalgia, that untenable myth of 'swinging London', as the yBa. In 1966, after the 'British invasion' spearheaded by the Beatles and the Stones, 'England' consolidated its 'victories' in two inter-imperialist wars by defeating the West German football team to win the world cup. 'Brit' chauvinists long for the feeling of consolidation events such as these give to their 'sense' of 'national identity', a 'Britishness' that has to be willed into being precisely because it never has and never will exist. And so, at the very moment the Anglo-American dominance of youth culture was threatened by the emergence of indigenous techno scenes in metropolitan 'centres' all over 'Europe', Blur and Oasis took up the 'axe' to do battle with the 'faceless' hordes of 'foreigners' autonomously creating their own dance music. 'British' culture can only go backwards, it's got nowhere else to go if the issue of cultural hybridity is to be avoided. The national identity currently being willed into being remains an echo of a non-existent 'white' past.

The cult of the personality is, of course, a central element in all totalitarian art. While both fascism and democracy are variants on the capitalist mode of economic organisation, the former adopts the political orator as its exalted embodiment of the 'great man,' while the latter opts for the artist. This distinction is crucial if one is to understand how the yBa is situated within the evolving discourse of totalitarian art. Had the 'bright young things' of the London gallery scene merely copied the cultural excesses of the Nazi era, their reactionary activities would have been ghettoised within the far-right fringe. However, the critics who theorise the yBa understand that by transforming art into a secular religion, rather than a mere adjunct of the state, liberalism imposes its domination over the 'masses' far more effectively than National Socialism. The focus, especially in the mass media, must be on the artists rather than the artwork.

What Roberts and his ilk are asking us to consume is a 'Britishness' rooted in sixties nostalgia, and that is therefore able to make much better use of the totalitarian obsession with 'youth' than more obviously 'volkish' productions. In this mythological realm, the seventies are dominated by punk, which the yBa has taken up precisely because punk has been rehistoricised as avant-garde art, rather than the popular culture it so obviously was and, in most cases, still is. For the unfortunate student of cultural studies, punk is a potlatch of sixties 'radicalism'. The importance of the situationists was hugely inflated in the construction of this revisionist history, which substituted London for Paris as the world centre of 'revolutionary' art, while the 'street' stood in for the coffee-house and the salon. Quasi-revolutionary rhetoric of the type indulged in by proponents of the 'punk as art' thesis, subsequently taken up by many of the apologists for the yBa, is part of a concerted attempt to divorce 'radicalism' from class analysis and simultaneously falsify history. Such phenomena have always been a feature of totalitarian discourse. Similarly, there is much talk of the yBa's 'clubbiness', a sly substitution for the notion of 'comradeship' found in less liberal forms of totalitarian culture, and one which simultaneously serves to retrench Anglo-American hegemony over youth culture in the face of its erosion within and through the techno explosion.

Now there is another element that is crucial to the success of totalitarian culture, and that is the factor of high kitsch. The words Stephen Crook uses to deal with the issue of fascism in his introduction to Theodor Adorno's *The Stars Down To Earth And Other Essays On The Irrational In Culture,* (Routledge, London and New York 1994) can very 'profitably' be applied to the yBa and the 'critical' apologists for those forms of totalitarian culture which have emerged within 'democratic' regimes:

> While its effects might be deadly, fascist propaganda is not altogether 'serious'... The audience who turn out to see and hear the fascist agitator expect a good show... Their 'sentimentality, blatant insincerity and phoniness' are not flaws in such performances, but the core of their appeal. The showman-like fakery of the agitator links him to the snake-oil salesman, the circus performer and an entire tradition of sentimentality and false tones... Even more than their originals, recent European fascisms are highly syncretic. German fascist youths parade in the costumes of British skinheads while carrying banners which imitate the swastika flag: theirs is a pastiche of fascism, but none the less dangerous for that.

One should not be surprised by the discrepancy between the high minded ideals 'traditionally' associated with art, and the subject matter that attracts totalitarian artists working under 'liberal' political conditions. Gilbert & George have their pictures of shit, just as Damien Hirst has worked with maggots. These serve to illustrate the gulf between art and life, a gulf which the totalitarian artist wishes to reinforce, whether it be through the idealised depiction of a Hitler or a Mao, or by the use of subject matter drawn from everyday life, which ceases to be ordinary after undergoing an 'alchemical' transformation through the medium of art. In fact, such discrepancies serve the totalitarian artist very well, since those who support work of this type expect blatant insincerity. Nevertheless, while Damien Hirst might be rated the sixth most irritating man in the world by *GQ Magazine,* hacks of this type only provide the main focus of attack for those who wish to strengthen, rather than undermine, the institution of art. Hirst, Bank, Gavin Turk *et al* are interchangeable in their irrelevance. An expert such as Roberts is quick to praise their "thinking stupidity" precisely because there is no danger of this crop of artists usurping the role of the critic by superseding art with philosophy.

Michael Archer, a less accomplished apologist for art than Roberts, concludes his yBa article *No Politics Please, We're British,* (*Art Monthly 194,* March 1996) with the observation that: "These people are making art, not theory." The social organisation of power under capitalism is predicated upon the canalisation of human activity into separate spheres. Within this system 'theory', or rather bourgeois ideology falsely claiming the status of theory, constitutes one of the major occult principles through which 'artists' and thus 'art objects' are materialised. Therefore it is the critics and curators who use the yBa to pursue the chauvinistic chimera of 'Britishness' whilst simultaneously retrenching class divisions, who I wish to make the focus of my attack. While 'English' intellectuals have never enjoyed the exalted status of their 'French' cousins, they are equally insidious and must be criticised from that materialist perspective which constantly reforges the passage between theory and practice, so that the great flood of human history may flow over the dikes erected by priests, cops, art critics and philosophers, washing away every discredited social form and thereby allowing the latent possibilities of this age to pour forth from the well-springs of human creativity.

Published in *everything 19,* May 1996

No more rock'n'roll

You've read the Kurt Cobain obituaries, now it's time to sit back and enjoy the ridiculous rumours circulating about the dead rock star. Personally, I think it's absurd to suggest the singer's suicide was faked. However, various cranks are claiming Cobain was gunned down by a hitman, possibly a member of the Mafia, who'd supposedly gone after Nirvana because the band refused to pay protection money.

Another version of the faked suicide story has Cobain alive and enjoying a break from the limelight. According to rumour, the singer has been popping up everywhere between Rio and Paris. London sightings include nights out at the Disobey Club, the Exploding Cinema and even the Hackney Homeless Festival. Most ludicrously of all, one fan claims to have clocked the rocker shopping at the Kwik Save supermarket in Canning Town.

A more believable theory about Cobain's death suggests he was the victim of a CIA mind control experiment. An individual claiming to represent "a private network of researchers" contacted me about this and arranged a meeting in the Temple Church on Fleet Street. Once I'd settled in a pew, a very nervous young man seated himself beside me. According to my contact, the CIA is deeply concerned about the subversive influence of popular music on young people, that's why "they murdered Brian Jones, John Lennon and Jim Morrison."

What's been worrying the spooks lately is the sway black radicalism has gained over the minds of white teenagers. To counter this "they've been pushing Nation of Islam style separatism among rappers." Likewise, the white Grunge movement spearheaded by Nirvana was backed by the CIA because "they wanted to divide youngsters on racial lines, if black and white kids linked up, they'd pose a serious threat to the system. The whole point of Grunge is to instil in teenagers a sense of hopelessness, to fill them with self-hate and prevent them changing the world."

Apparently, the CIA got hold of Cobain when he was still unknown, then using drugs, hypnosis and medical torture, they broke his will and rebuilt his personality. "Most of the time he'd act relatively normal," I was told, "but all it took was a few key words spoken over the phone and Cobain would carry out the deeds he'd been programmed to enact." My contact was convinced that the singer had been brainwashed into committing suicide at the peak of his success because the CIA figured this would reduce his potentially rebellious fans to complete despair. However, the conspiracy theorist admitted several of his fellow researchers thought Cobain had taken his own life as the only means of breaking free from the influence of his controllers. If this is the case, then the rock star is a hero rather than simply a victim, and his death provides grounds for a fresh outbreak of teenage rebellion.

First published in *Underground 4,* Summer 1994

ROYAL WATCH:
THE ERA OF WORLD RUIN!

THE COLD WAR between the House of Windsor and the Vatican is heating up with the media reporting that the Princess of Wales has been flirting with Catholicism. Investigations by the Neoist Alliance have revealed that Diana was recruited by the Jesuits prior to her marriage. The calamities presently befalling the royal family are part of a sting operation whose origins date back in time to the British backed assassination of JFK in the 1963 Dallas 'turkey shoot'. The Vatican had hoped that installing a Catholic president would be the first step towards re-establishing the Holy Roman Empire with Washington becoming the third and final Rome.

Using their lackeys in the American Council On Foreign Relations, during the sixties the Windsors systematically smashed the Papacy's power base in North America. The Vatican retaliated by rearming its IRA foot soldiers and instructing them to wage war against the British in Northern Ireland. However, what they really wanted was control of the British mainland. To this end, the Jesuits recruited moles among the English upper classes. Clearly, Diana and Fergie were among the most important of these secret converts, but it's impossible to evaluate the extent of Papal penetration into the British establishment until we know the identity of the mysterious 'third babe'.

Obviously, most 'Protestant' commentators have failed to grasp the significance of the possible shattering of the Act of Settlement of 1701 which banned Catholic monarchs from occupying the British throne and their heirs from marrying Papists. Writing in *The London Review of Books* (19 August 1993), Linda Colley asks "how are loyal Protestant subjects of Northern

Ireland going to react to a Catholic King Billy?" Talk of this type is highly misleading because if Diana smashes the Act of Settlement by bringing her children up as Catholics, it means the end of the British state.

There is little likelihood of the British being ruled by a single Catholic king. If the bar on Catholic monarchs is lifted, Prince Albrecht of Bavaria is first in line for the English throne, while William will get to rule the Welsh. Contenders too numerous to mention have long been vying for the principalities of Scotland, Kernow, Mannin and Ulster. For the time being, the Jesuit plot to destroy the Neo-British Empire looks more likely to succeed than the crumbling Maastrict programme being pushed by the Hanseatic League. If the Jesuit plan reaches fruition, Diana will be crowned Queen of Bohemia as a reward for her loyalty to the Papal cause.

Ultimately, the Vatican aims to dominate Europe using Prague as the centre of its operations. Rather unsurprisingly, it's the Hapsburgs who'd front a revived Holy Roman Empire. Rumours circulating among Protestant insiders suggest that the monarchy is planning to hit back by revealing its adherence to various Pagan cults. While the English press spent much of the early eighties 'deriding' the belief Prince Charles expressed in reincarnation, it never went as far as speculating on who the future king believed himself to have been in previous lives.

Charlie has extremely vivid memories of having been incarnated as a world leader who died just a few years before he was born. Yes, our would-be ruler believes that in a previous life he was Adolf Hitler! Charles also claims to have 'come back' as both Genghis Khan and Akhmaton (the Egyptian king who instituted monotheistic worship of the sun). The Windsors want to abandon the concept of a royal bloodline and instead foist a series of charismatic dictators on their 'subjects'. They're hoping the public will endure their ongoing misrule if it can be persuaded that this change of tack is actually a return to traditional Saxon conceptions of monarchy!

The City of London is less than happy with Charlie's planned counter-attack against the Vatican. As a consequence, representatives of the Mercers and Drapers Guilds have been conducting secret negotiations with the Hanseatic League. These meetings have shocked all those familiar with the deeds of the Gresham family who set up the stock exchange and are known to posterity as 'the hammer of the Hansa'. However, City leaders see rapprochement with the Hanseatic League as the only means of preserving Europe's Sufi-cum-Protestant traditions. As far as the Guilds are concerned, a line has to be drawn between them and Catholic idolatry. Now that the monarchy has been infiltrated by the Jesuits, it looks as if London is about to disown the corrupt political apparatus centred on Westminster. It has long been accepted that the 'head' of the British state is required to surrender their sword when entering Fleet Street from the Strand. It may not be long before the Corporation of London demands that the rest of the population produces a passport when travelling in and out of the 'Square Mile'. You have been warned!

First published in *Underground 3*, Autumn 1993

NODDY CRUCIFIED:
A DAVID TIBET INTERVIEW

DAVID TIBET needs no introduction to his hardcore cult following, and yet he remains an enigma to many of his fans. Tibet looks every bit the master of the house as he lounges in a study sipping chilled wine and playing with his eight cats as they wander in and out of the room. On the wall are original Wain and Spare paintings, while rare first editions are neatly arranged on various bookshelves. Tibet has come a long way since his early days with Psychic TV and Dogs Blood Rising; he's dropped out of the sights of the rock press who viewed him as Satan incarnate, with the majority of those purchasing Current 93 product now perceiving him as a deeply religious man. A bright spring morning is in the process of being eclipsed by an afternoon of torrential rain as I press the record button on my Walkman.

Home: Okay Mr. Tibet, I'd like you to tell me about your belief in Christ. Do you see Christ as the Son of God or do you see him as a master who has been reincarnated?

Tibet: I conceive of Christ as the Son of God. That's not to say he's the only one. In Christianity, Christ has to be seen as genetically, as it were, connected to the Father, as opposed to someone like Manson who claimed he was the Son of God in an inspirational sense. I think that the Christian claim that Christ is the Son of God means that there is a special relationship which is beyond inspiration. Christ is, as He claimed, the Son of God, but other people are the Sons of God as well.

Home: How would you relate that to Free Spirit heresies, the belief that if God is everywhere, then we are all part of God and, in fact, must be God ourselves.

Tibet: I think the Free Spirit were right. I think people have a lot of problems with what I say because they see me as either a Crowleyite, or as a Buddhist, or as a Christian, because of the mingling of imagery in my songs. Crowleyanity and Thelema were certainly something I was connected with in the past, but I don't have any interest in them now beyond the fact that I still have a sense of humour, so I do still like to flick through Crowley's books.

Home: I think Christianity is a syncretic religion, what are your views on this?

Tibet: In terms of influences on it, Christianity is certainly syncretic, but then I think every religion is syncretic, nothing starts up totally in a vacuum. Apart from the obvious Judaistic elements in Christianity, then you can have Hellenism, Buddhism, anything you want really. Likewise, it depends on what you mean by Christianity. Our knowledge of the early Church is limited to basically what the early Church said about itself and allowed to be put in print, so other views of the early Church have been destroyed. I think what Christianity did do, which for me made it very different to other religions, was to say there is no need for an intermediary between you and God; that man has been made free and that the old laws have been broken.

Home: That's very much a Protestant view; within Catholicism there's a tradition of praying to Mary or various Saints rather than directly to God.

Tibet: In terms of popular devotion that may be true but the Catholic Church would never say you should pray to Mary rather than Christ, or that Mary is higher than Christ. Doctrinally Mary is definitely under Christ, if that's not too blasphemous a way of expressing the point.

Home: In practice most Catholics tend to pray to Mary or one of the Saints, and some people would say that was the influence of pagan Goddess worship on Catholicism.

Tibet: That would obviously seem to be the case. It's a similar thing with Buddhism, people in the West look at Buddhism and they say it's an incredibly pure doctrine. Western converts often don't view Buddhism as a religion. Theoretically, in a Buddhist country, especially a Hinayana Buddhist country, the idea is that you're not meant to pray to Buddha, there are no Gods, all of this is the play of the mind, reality is hidden from us by illusion. But if you actually go to a Buddhist country, you'd find people praying to the local snake deity and the Buddha that protects against small pox. You can't find a pure expression of religious theory anywhere or even a pure theory. In any case, there isn't a pure dogma because Saint Thomas Aquinas will disagree with Saint Augustine. Likewise, after the Reformation and Counter-Reformation you've got completely divergent views on the nature of Christ. The most impressive thing I've ever read on the paradox that is Christianity is in the *Pensées,* where Pascal writes that Christ is in agony until the end of the world and we must not rest in the meantime. That is a pure statement of the patripassionist[1] heresy. What most fascinates me in post-Gnostic Christianity is the idea that when Christ was crucified time actually stopped and that real time, in as far as that has any meaning, has been frozen, and that we're living through the death throes of Christ. As soon as Christ has died on the Cross the world is ended, so that in a way as soon as the first nails were knocked in, time itself stopped and the last few seconds or minutes or hours of Christ's agony, everything that's happened since the nailing happens in that frozen moment of time. The idea here is that Christ's agony has either frozen time or that our experience is being packed into the very short space of time related to the agony on the Cross.

Home: I'm interested in this idea that I find in some of your work that Christ has reincarnated and walks amongst us again, although perhaps reincarnation isn't really the right turn of phrase.

Tibet: I think reincarnation is a difficult issue. G. K. Chesterton, a fairly orthodox convert to Rome, said that reincarnation was not against the spirit of the Catholic Church, although obviously the Catholic Church teaches that reincarnation is not acceptable. Reincarnation, metempsychosis, transmigration, are all concepts that even Buddhists have difficulty explaining because as long as we're connected to our ego, descriptions of egoless states are hard for us to comprehend. My belief in Christ's return is connected to another belief that I've always had, and that I enunciated on the very first Current 93 album *Nature Unveiled.* I think we are living in the End Days and that Christ has returned and is actually amongst us. I'm not saying that I'm a member of Benjamin Creme's party, and I'm not saying that the Son of God is called Maitreya, but I do think Christ has returned. Teilhard de Chardin said that Christ has actually returned and is permeating the world. Chardin claimed that Christ is not in one body yet. It's a bit like before a thunderstorm, the particles are charged and then suddenly they come together and there's a lightning flash, but just before that bright flash all the particles are preparing for that vital moment. I agree with Chardin's belief.

Home: So, the notion of *Hitler As Kalki,* how does that relate to your belief that Christ has returned?

Tibet: I explained *Hitler As Kalki* in some sleeve notes, although as usual a lot of people misunderstood it. A couple of morons wrote to me and asked me how I could praise Hitler in this way. It gob-smacked me really, they obviously had no grasp of English and didn't bother reading the liner notes.

Home: If I recall correctly, you dedicated that song to your father, who fought Hitler in the last world war.

Tibet: Yeah, I gave *Thunder Perfect Mind* to dad and he said "thank you very much," because in the picture of the soldiers, the one with the curly hair at the front is my father. He said to look at it you'd think that he'd fought Hitler single-handedly and pursued him into the Bunker. As I said in the sleeve notes, in the Hindu view of things, Vishnu incarnates ten times in each world cycle. A world cycle takes place when Brahma awakes; when he closes his eyes and sleeps then the world is destroyed. When he wakes from his sleep the world is recreated, *ad infinitum*. Vishnu in this cycle of Brahma's waking incarnates on earth ten times. His final incarnation is as Kalki, a white man on a horse holding a blazing sword with only two arms and one head, which is unusual for Hindu iconography. Hitler seems to me to represent the position of Kalki; Hitler basically destroyed the world and we're now living in the apocalyptic landscape. Just as I believe that Christ has returned, I believe that Hitler was an incarnation of Vishnu as Kalki, I believe that Hitler was Anti-Christ. Although, just as I believe there are other Sons of God apart from Christ, I believe that there are other Anti-Christs. If you look at the *Little Apocalypse* in *Daniel* and the main *Apocalypse* in *John,* and also in Paul's *Letters,* there are differing views about what Anti-Christ is. People consider Anti-Christ to be a major figure who arises at the end of the world to battle Christ, but many Anti-Christs will arise, anyone who acts against the spirit of Christ is Anti-Christ. *Daniel* seems to imply that several Anti-Christs will arise with the Last World Emperor, and the Beast, and the Dragon, these are perhaps all types of Anti-Christ. Hitler was an Anti-Christ, I think Hitler was an unwitting incarnation of Vishnu, as the sign to say that this is the end of the world. But that's not to say that we'll see the end of the world in our life-times, I'm not sure about that, I'd rather we didn't.

Home: Given your interest in religion, I find it curious that you don't utilise Islam in your work, particularly Sufism, although I can see that you might have problems with the crucial Islamic assertion that 'there is no god but God, and His name is Allah.'

Tibet: I'm not particularly interested in Islam; there are interesting things in that religion but I'm not trying to make a synthesis of religions. I've got an intellectual interest in all religions, more or less. However, in terms of my own emotional response, I'm really only interested in Christianity and Buddhism, and Hinduism to a certain degree. That may well be because of my childhood, being brought up in Asia. I'm also attracted to Chinese popular religion, not Taoism *per se* but the odd selection of Gods you find in Taoist

Temples. Historically, Islam was never very strong in Malaysia, although it is now more of an Islamic country. I think you can find everything that is in Sufism in Christianity, and everything that's in Christianity is in Buddhism, and ditto with all religions. I think the problem now is that people don't look at religion as a spiritual path to enlightenment or to merging one's soul in the Godhead, or whatever you want to call it. People are too inclined to look on religion as some kind of fashion choice. Individuals shouldn't practice Islam or Buddhism or Christianity because it looks good, or because they like the deities, or because it's weird and it's hip. I think the problem with the magickal path and how it differentiates from the religious path, is that people seem so intent on personal power that they never consider how this might benefit humanity as a whole. It's me, me, me, me, me. Whereas, if there is a reason for the spiritual path, it's certainly not just for the aggregation of power to yourself because you will still die no matter how much power or money or how many Louis Wain paintings you aggregate, and you can't take that with you. Similarly, occultists so rarely have a sense of humour. Crowley was renowned for having a great sense of humour, even if it was often at other people's expense. Likewise, sex magick is popularly perceived to be the essence of Crowleyanity, but most of the people I've met who claim to follow this path don't appear to be getting laid at all. It reminds me of schoolboys singing songs about shagging fourteen birds in the shower, when they're still in fact virgins. So I discard occultism utterly, although I think a Celtic Scientology or an Odinist Moonie movement would be good. However, for me, the central question is what is the nature of our continuity after death if, indeed, there's any. We may just be out like a light and that's it.

Home: A lot of your use of religious imagery, appears very personal to you.

Tibet: I've always felt that the religious ideas I enunciate are just my personal feelings about these things; I've never claimed that they are ideas that other people should share. They are my personal reaction. I've always thought of myself as having an apocalyptic mentality; I tend to see endings in everything, far more, unfortunately, than rebirths. I see apocalypse all around us, which makes me a somewhat pessemistic person. As a consequence, I experience no difficulties in holding both Christian and Buddhist beliefs; I'm not formulating a synthesis of religions. There are ideas that I hold very strongly and that I believe are completely true. My beliefs about Christ having returned, and the Apocalypse, and Hitler being Kalki, I think are completely correct in terms of my own personal reality, but I'm not saying that this is a reality that holds good for everyone. I think people are becoming increasingly aware that there are alternate realities and manifold worlds, and that there are as many of these as there are people existing who believe in them.

Home: You don't appear interested in imposing a single response to your work among your audience.

Tibet: I'm not trying to impose any ideas on my audience. I'm not interested in what they think about what I think. The music is solely a reflection of the way I feel about things. There's no message for anyone.

Home: When I listen to your CDs, one of the things I'm often tempted to do is treat them as novelty records.

Tibet: Thank you. Do you listen to the Chipmunks after playing Current 93?

Home: No, I prefer the Pork Dukes or Shampoo. Seriously though, I have a great love of novelty records and to me, if I put on a Crass album, that's a novelty record because the ideology they're pushing is so absurd. While Crass appear to be very serious about what they're saying, I find their ideology hilarious because it is completely unworkable.

Tibet: It works in a personal community but unfortunately not on a global scale.

Home: Anyway, one way in which I listen to some of your output is as novelty songs. For example, whenever I put on *Crowleymass Unveiled* I just fall about laughing.

Tibet: That song is meant to be a joke.

Home: Are you worried about whether people consume your music as a vehicle for serious religious messages or whether they treat the lyrics as a joke? Are you concerned about what people are taking from your work?

Tibet: The only person who could really understand any record that I've done is myself, whereas Crass, who I admire greatly, were obviously positing some sort of way of looking at the world that it would be good if people shared. I certainly don't believe that people should share my view of the patripassionist nature of reality, or the idea that Hitler is Kalki. It might well be good for them to think of ideas that I hold to be true, only in as much as it will broaden their outlook by taking in any idea, just as I broaden my outlook by listening to what other people have to say. Some people will sympathise with my world view, some people will find it ludicrous. but that doesn't matter in the slightest. I think personal belief is very important, but projecting these beliefs onto others is the root of many problems. Once you've got ideology or dogma, everything breaks down and people lose their souls.

Home: I want to move on to your use of childhood imagery, Louis Wain cats and Noddy, and your blending of this with very apocalyptic religious imagery. Is there any theory behind this synthesis, or is it just something that occurs?

Tibet: It's something that has been with me since childhood. Certainly there wasn't any theory behind it originally, because I don't think you're enunciating theories to yourself when you're very young. As a child I was always very interested in extreme politics and extreme religious beliefs. I was apocalyptic, as it were, from a very early age. A close friend once said that the symbol I use a lot of Noddy crucified is an archetype of innocence betrayed. When I was very young, I had a lot of very unpleasant experiences, particularly at my schools but at the same time, my childhood, particularly when I was in Malaysia, was when I was most happy. After I was sent away from Malaysia at the age of ten, although I returned for holidays, I was never happy again. There are moments of happiness, but in a way being sent away from Malaysia destroyed my life, so I suppose all the figures I empathise with are people who've had their innocence destroyed at a very early age. We all go back to childhood, again and again, that's when we were formed and we never lose the obsessions that we got when we were young. I'm not interested in sophistication. Current 93's music is very simple, there's usually a very basic theme that's elaborated and a basic statement of my belief or a basic story told. I think that the apocalyptic message that interests me says that all your sophistication is as nought, that all of this will be destroyed and that all that will remain is the essence. I don't think you can ever come to terms with obsessions or ride them out. If they happen at an early age, they're so imprinted on your psyche that you can't do anything about them. They're there, you can't bring them to the surface and let them go in the way that therapists claim will happen under their analysis. In Scientology they call this an engram, it's an imprint, you can't get rid of it. It is your personal, pubescent, karma.

At this point tea was ready, and so the interview came to an end. I settled down in front of the telly with Tibet and his girlfriend Kat, to eat pasta and salad. Outside, it was still pissing with rain.

First published in *On: The World And Everything In It 1*, Spring 1997

1: Douglas, Elwell and Toon in their *Concise Dictionary of Christian Tradition: Worship, Liturgy & History* (Marshall Pickering, London 1989), define patripassionism as: "the doctrine that God the Father actively suffered on the cross of Jesus. The word was used by critics of those who taught Modalism or Sebellianism and who believed that God is One who appears in three forms (Father, Son and Spirit) but is not really three persons." Please note that this is only one among a number of possible definitions of patripassionism, and it is included here simply as a rough guide to the idea. Tibet's understanding of the term is clearly somewhat different to that of Douglas, Elwell and Toon.

WHY 400,000 PEOPLE ARE WRONG

THE RECENT CRAZE for blockbuster retrospectives harks back to art's nineteenth-century heyday, when people would queue for hours to catch a glimpse of work by John Martin and other then popular painters. What with Cézanne at the Tate, Corot in Paris, Vermeer at The Hague and Degas about to open at the National Gallery in London, it has been claimed that art exhibitions now have more spectators than football matches. However, since the average visitor to an art show spends less than a minute in front of each painting, it's doubtful many are gaining any real sense of aesthetic delectation from the works they come to view.

Blockbusters are promoted as events of immense pomp and significance, but the reality is an unpleasant stampede through packed galleries. The hype attracts those veterans of the Oxford Street sales, the bargain hunting middle classes. These people aren't really interested in art, they're simply rising to the challenge of a mega-queue. The crush at a jumble sale palls in comparison to the crowds attracted by blockbusters. And if you think its hard work viewing the pictures, the exhibition proper won't fully prepare you for the scrum in the souvenir shop.

Art critic Nick Houghton has no time for blockbusters: "These shows are the equivalent of Hollywood films, massively hyped and designed to a formula. What they suggest is a sort of fast food culture, where the big names of art are delivered up for mass consumption. Increasingly art shows are defined by sponsorship. You have to get a neat package together to get the corporate money. We are heading for a situation where sponsors define the state of our institutional culture. A lot of art professionals disagree with blockbusters but are too worried about their jobs to say anything." As Houghton suggests, off the record a number of curators were willing to tell me that they abhorred blockbusters, but they all insisted their views weren't for public consumption.

Three art students I met in the Tate were more forthcoming: "blockbusters are too expensive. Besides, we're not interested in that old stuff." After doing Cézanne, one of 408,000 visitors complained to me: "They shouldn't let so many people in at once – it was far too crowded. I think it's a real shame most people aren't bothering to go and look at the rest of the Tate gallery. They have some really brilliant paintings here, but it's obvious that most people just came to see Cézanne, which gives you the feeling that they're acting like sheep."

Artists aren't keen on blockbusters either. John Fare is an itinerant cultural terrorist in his mid-forties, whose partially sighted girlfriend leads him around art shows blindfolded: "I just stand in front of the paintings and tell anyone who asks that I'm taking in the aura. If I'm not getting a reaction, I ask people which picture I'm looking at" he says. "I'm not liked in the artworld. When I went to New York, I was thrown out of exhibitions for touching the canvases and taking off my clothes. I didn't get it – I'd be in these rooms filled with nudes and people were offended when I stripped off. I don't do that now – these days I'm into a more subtle thing. I went to Cézanne and I'll be going to Degas. I want to upset people's expectations about what happens in an art gallery."

With his ripped and dirty clothing, Fare will stand out like a sore thumb among the crowd who flock to see Degas. While middle-aged women in their Marks and Sparks best might not understand Fare's desire to undermine 'consensus reality', they are far more likely to see the funny side of his blindfolded visit than those artworld insiders who dismiss his performance work as a juvenile prank.

The public seem to take little notice of the critics. While press reports stressed the showbiz-style hype accompanying blockbusters, the punters rarely mention it. "I like the pictures," was a common refrain among those who'd acquired one of the strictly rationed tickets for Cézanne. The people I spoke to were happy to pay for the pleasure of viewing paintings that they were already familiar with. Degas at the National might actually disappoint this type of art lover because, unlike the inclusive nature of the Cézanne show, it concentrates on his lesser-known works.

Fare's antics may not be subtle, but he is making a valid point. People approach art wearing blinkers – they don't want to be confronted by anything challenging. Blockbuster shows are a symptom of a sick culture. During art's nineteenth-century heyday, vast crowds of people queued to see new works – that doesn't happen anymore. Instead we're still being packed in to see the same old things.

First published in *The Big Issue 181,* 13-19 May 1996

THE ALABAMA 3
DO SEX MAGICK WITH A GROUPIE

WHEN I LAST SPOKE to Jake Black of the Alabama 3, he was making extravagant claims about his role in the death of Princess Diana. Styling himself The Very Reverend Dr D. Wayne Love of the First Presleyterian Church Of Elvis The Divine (UK), Jake plonked a dozen copies of his church newsletter *Loving You* in my hand before hollering "spread the word." I wasn't sure whether Reverend Love wanted me to write about his 'new outlaw acid' grooves, the black magick with which he'd hexed Diana, or merely to circulate copies of his church newsletter. Months later, a set of photographs featuring yours truly, some female friends and a lot of whipped cream, were used to persuade me that I wanted to witness an occult attack on the royals. This necessitated spending hogmanay with Black, a heavily tattooed Hell's Angel called The Book Of Love and the renowned groupie DJ Bird.

We travelled to Stonehaven, a small town in north-east Scotland, by car. We arrived about nine at night on New Year's Eve and piled into a pub. Jake, The Book Of Love and I downed several pints of heavy. DJ Bird managed the best part of a half. The groupie spent most of her time harassing Reverend Love for lines of charlie, which she snorted in the ladies. The pub closed at eleven and, like everyone else, we headed for the High Street where the Fireballs Ceremony was taking place. Jake positioned himself behind some barriers very close to the harbour, then handed The Book Of Love a Hi-8 camera and proceeded to fiddle about with various tape recorders.

It wasn't long before the little street was packed with six thousand spectators. One of the worst pipe bands I have ever heard marched up and down; they'd had so much to drink that they could barely keep time and abandoned their performance after less than ten minutes. The piping over, forty or so nutters began lighting wire balls. These were filled with paraffin soaked wood and cloth, and had been attached to pieces of cable so that those taking part in the ceremony could whirl the flaming things above their heads. Jake and The Book of Love recorded the fireball swingers as they marched up and down the High Street before throwing their fireballs into the harbour. The ceremony lasted half an hour and I took care to stand well back, since a bunch of drunks swinging balls of flame around their heads is extremely dangerous. This fake pagan custom is supposed to ward off evil spirits. It originated as a fisherman's festival and assumed its present form about 150 years ago.

As the crowd dispersed, we returned to our car and headed inland towards Banchory on the A597. We parked outside the town at the base of a hill named Scolty. Our ascent of the hill was rather slow until we stopped half way up and Jake gave DJ Bird a couple of lines of coke to help her on her way. At the summit there is a stone tower originally erected around the same time as the Stonehaven hogmanay celebrations took on an overtly pagan form. After falling derelict, the tower was refurbished before being re-opened by Prince Charles in 1992. Reverend Love and his assistant DJ Bird were going to perform some sex magick at the top, which Jake claimed would prevent Chaz from ever becoming king. The tower had been selected as the site for this ceremony precisely because of its association with the heir to the throne. The Book Of Love was there to document the ritual on video, while I was acting as a witness from the press.

We climbed the steel stairs to the tiny platform just below the top of the open tower. Reverend Love and DJ Bird undressed and felt each other up. I stood on the steps beneath The Book Of Love and had to crane my neck to see what was going on. As Jake and DJ Bird got it on, I played back random selections from the audio recordings that had been made earlier that evening.

The idea, as far as I understood it, was to direct the energy released during the Fireballs Ceremony against Prince Charles. Reverend Love pumped away on top of DJ Bird while simultaneously chanting the names Satan, Lucifer, Belial, Leviathan and Elvis. After a while, Jake stood up and DJ Bird gave head while he squawked these names over and over again. Eventually, Reverend Love took his assistant up her Gary Glitter and his five word mantra was wailed a great many more times.

Arse shagging is said to be the most powerful form of sex magick and the platform was shaking away as Jake shot his wad into DJ Bird's derrière. Once he'd recovered, Reverend Love told me that the final part of the ritual required that I go down on the groupie while he performed a special invocation. I demanded some custard, and this request left Jake and The Book Of Love somewhat bemused. Spelling it out, I explained that if I was going to eat, I wanted custard tart. Taking this to be a blunt refusal on my part to participate in the ritual, The Book Of Love handed me his Hi-8 camera and said I should do the filming while he exercised his tongue. Reverend Love struck a bizarre pose and shrieked the most peculiar mixture of Latin and Glaswegian doggerel I'd heard in my entire life. Jake followed this up by throwing his arms about and cursing in a dozen different languages.

Several different cassette tapes of the Stonehaven celebrations were blasting out as Jake closed the ritual. Elvis posters were placed at strategic points as we made our way down the stairs, and a doll dressed up to resemble the singer was left at the entrance to the tower. We made our way to the car and drove to a bed and breakfast that was open over hogmanay. DJ Bird lapsed into unconsciousness before we arrived, and The Book Of Love had to carry her up to bed. Fortunately, she recovered sufficiently to eat a hearty fry-up in the morning. As for Chaz, if Reverend Love knows half as much about magick as he claims, then Big Ears has had his chips.

First published in *Sunshine 3*, Winter 1998

ROYAL WATCH: ANTI-CHRIST UNVEILED

AS WE RUSH HEADLONG towards the millennium, Prince Charles is preparing to reveal to a stunned world that he is the reincarnation of Adolf Hitler. Having spent years promoting 'socialist' and 'green' ideas, the maverick royal is now emphasising the reactionary elements of his political ideology by attacking 'trendy' theories of child care and espousing other conservative causes. As a dedicated Nazi, Charles is a demagogue who mixes elements from the 'left' and the 'right' in his speeches, thus it should not surprise anyone that he has come out in favour of spanking children. As the *Sunday Times* of 8 May 1994 euphemistically put it, Charles is "a paternalistic landowner with a highly developed sense of *noblesse oblige.*" In other words, he's a fully fledged collectivist who has embraced the 'romantic' politics of the far-right. It's only a matter of time before the issue of 'fascistic royalism' as a 'beneficent' force is openly raised in the 'quality' press.

Charles shares Hitler's belief in the occult and is impatient to ascend to the throne so that he can openly impose a dictatorship across the entire span of the European continent. Since his mother shows no sign of abdicating, the Prince intends to have her ritually sacrificed on 6 February 1997, exactly forty-five years after the death of his grandfather. In doing this, Charles is following the nine year cycle that was the customary period for Divine King slaughter in his family's native Germany. In England, the cycle is by tradition based on periods of seven years. Charles intends to be crowned King before his fiftieth birthday, in the very year that Gresham College, the 'Invisible College' of the Rosicrucians, celebrates its four hundredth anniversary. The Queen will, of course, be strangled with the customary 'string,' and that notorious multiple coven, the Order of the Garter, will fall under the absolute command of the Prince-cum-King.

Richard Chartres, the Bishop of Stepney, is preparing to take the place of the ageing Laurens van der Post as the Prince's principal psychic advisor. As such, it is the Bishop who will do the honours when the Queen is killed. Chartres, who opposed the ordination of wimmin priests, is now a top member of the 'Anglo-Catholic' London movement that has been holding secret meetings to 'save' the Church of England from disintegration. The Chartres family take their name from the French town whose Cathedral is known to openly display the secrets of the Philosopher's Stone in its gargoyles, glyphs, rose windows and flying buttresses. The Bishop has, of course, been initiated into the esoteric science of reading these symbols. This cleric is set to become the next Archbishop of Canterbury after making an agreement with the Prince that he will act as a substitute Divine Victim in 2006, just as Thomas a Becket stood in for Henry II in 1170.

Like Charles, Chartres is a pagan who has adopted the trappings of Christianity as a show designed to deceive the masses. *East End Life* of 12 May 1994 quoted the Bishop as saying "prayer is not a soft option, it supplies energy for change." This 'slip' demonstrates quite clearly that Chartres does not believe in Christian dogma, which asserts that prayer is a way of calling upon God to intercede in the world. Like all occultists, the Bishop believes that his magickal powers give him direct control over the forces of nature. During the course of his lectures as Gresham Professor of Divinity, Chartres was completely free to speak about his cabbalistic beliefs. What's astounding is his willingness to expound on these heretical views in a local newspaper now that he sits in the House of Lords.

The Bishop has made no secret of his plan to build a 'church' or Temple in the pyramid that tops the Canary Wharf Tower, and it's also well known that, through its Royal Society front, Gresham College controls so called 'chaos magick'. A contributor to issue 15 of the journal *Chaos International* wrote of visualising "a Chaos Temple dedicated to Siva" in the Canary Wharf pyramid, at a time when the Bishop was still a Gresham professor. Clearly, this dupe's activities were being guided by the hidden hand of Chartres, although the 'chaos magickian' insanely imagines that the Canary Wharf project went bankrupt as a result of his 'creative visualisation'. This bozo is a rank amateur whose 'powers' pale in comparison to those of the top professionals who run the British establishment, and like his associates in the 'occult' underground, he is in no position to resist their commands.

From all this it should be clear that Chartres is even more accomplished as a Magus than van der Post. With the Bishop on his side, Charles is an unstoppable force unless the evil plot to impose an occult theocracy across the entire span of the European continent is widely exposed. The masses must rise up in revolt against 'their' rulers and drag the bastards kicking and screaming to the nearest cross-roads, where stakes should be hammered through their black hearts. It's pointless to support Elizabeth against her son; to achieve freedom we must overthrow the monarchy and wipe out the aristocracy before these scum-suckers openly proclaim themselves to be a Fourth Reich.

First published in *Underground 4,* Summer 1994

DRILLER KILLER

BEN WATSON IS A JEKYLL AND HYDE CHARACTER. Under the alias Out To Lunch he is one of the craziest chancers to be found beyond the outer fringes of rumour on the small press poetry scene. As Ben Watson he is a respected music critic who turns up regularly on Radio 4 talking about cutting edge culture. Extremely weird shit starts flying whenever these two personas become mixed up, as happened in both *Frank Zappa: The Negative Dialectics Of Poodle Play* and Watson's new book *Art, Class & Cleavage: A Quantulumcunque Concerning Materialist Esthetix*. The former resulted in Watson being described as loaded with more brain candy than the gonzoid rock journalist Hunter S. Thompson. The latter consolidates his reputation as the wittiest street seller of the *Socialist Worker* agitational broadsheet.

Whatever you think of Watson's unfashionable opinions, he's certainly got a lot of bottle. A couple of years ago I saw him lecturing an audience of hostile anarchists on the crucial role the Socialist Workers Party had played in the development of revolutionary theory. Since this event took place at The Hacienda in Manchester, Fall singer Mark E. Smith was the most persistent and drunken heckler. Watson ploughed through to the end of his talk quite unperturbed by the hatred he'd aroused. He continues his propaganda crusade on behalf of the SWP in *Art, Class & Cleavage,* a book that combines political and aesthetic positions that many perceive as incompatible. In view of this, Watson's ability to find a commercial publisher for polemics that are rarely encountered outside small press pamphlets is particularly remarkable.

Having heard that Watson's forehead would be drilled open at the launch of *Art, Class & Cleavage,* I hot footed it to Compendium Books on Camden High Street. As I arrived, a big guy with shoulder length hair was being ejected from the private party for distributing copies of the *Socialist Wiccan Newsletter.* As I understand it, Socialist Wiccan is a secret network, with links to the pagan and revolutionary scenes, which developed after a number of expulsions from the Southampton branch of the SWP. The purged activists got involved with an anarchist group, while those who survived rigorous investigation secretly formed Socialist Wiccan. The SWP does not allow internal factions so a clandestine tendency which campaigns for the study and celebration of the cosmic wheel is a matter of considerable concern to its leadership.

Once I'd pushed my way into Compendium, I found the novelist and psychogeographer Iain Sinclair reading a piece he'd written especially for the occasion: "Watson writes in a trance, revolution is his medium. He laces his prose with the initials SWP because such placements are a red rag to his detractors. He is a photographic negative and when the literal meanings of his writings are reversed, they gain prophetic infallibility. Watson is dealing in automatic writing, table tapping, ouija boards. Read backwards his poetry becomes the most reasonable approximation of the truth. Misheard asides mature into full-blown rumours. Pub whispers infiltrate gossip columns, then feed back to the SWP hierarchy. Impossible to say who funds Watson, who invented him or if he actually exists as anything other than a regiment of clones and imitators."

After Sinclair finished his set, Watson got up and read a section of his new book which he'd entitled 'DIY Schizophrenia'. It describes events in 1984 when Out To Lunch was prescribed largatil by his GP before being sectioned in Highroyds Mental Hospital. It was at this time that he became convinced schizophrenia was an ideological rather than a medical problem. The SWP was his self-prescribed cure, a rigid structure that gave shape and discipline to his thoughts at a time when he was unable to distinguish between 'essence' and 'appearance'. In the persona of Out To Lunch, he describes playing records to the TV test card as a form of psychic warfare against fascists who were trying to transform the black patch at the centre of the screen into a swastika. As part of the political left, Out To Lunch wanted to let colour flow freely again.

Watson ended his reading by removing his prescription spectacles and putting on a pair of sunglasses. He sat down on a chair and the shades were taped to his face. Out To Lunch's assistant Esther Leslie explained that this was to prevent blood getting into Ben's eyes as she drilled through his forehead. Watson was about to undergo trepanation. According to proponents of the operation, a small hole drilled into the forehead allows the brain to pulsate fully and thus improves all mental functions. Trepanation was pioneered by Dr. Bart Hughes, who was active in Amsterdam countercultural circles during the sixties. Hughes developed the operation during the course of experiments with LSD and yoga. While Watson is sceptical about the effectiveness of this practice, he wanted to prove that it was not mere squeamishness that led him to advocate SWP membership as a more radical and mentally liberating option.

Esther Leslie used layers of elastoplast to mark out a small spot on Watson's forehead very close to his hairline. She picked up a dentist's drill and set to work making a tiny hole in Watson's skull. Several individuals at the back of the room had chattered through the earlier readings but even they fell silent as the drill whirled and blood streamed down Watson's face. The operation only took a couple of minutes. Once Esther had dressed the wound she'd made during the trepanation, a white dove was released from a wicker basket. It flapped about the bookshop until someone held open the door so that the bird could fly out. The book launch was over and most of those present wandered along to the Oxford Arms where they continued drinking.

I bought Watson a pint and asked him how he felt. He said he had a migraine but that it was nothing compared to the headache Tony Blair faced once the SWP got the entire working class mobilised against the capitalist state.

First published in *D>Tour*, March 1998

ABOUT THE HISTORIFICATION
OF THE SITUATIONIST INTERNATIONAL

Ralph Rumney in conversation with Stewart Home, Paris 7 April 1989.

Home: I'm curious to know how you feel about a Situationist exhibition being held at the Centre Georges Pompidou and the Institute Of Contemporary Arts.

Rumney: My feelings are rather mixed. We held protests against the Stedelijk and the Triennalle because we wanted to do our own thing. That was a long time ago. What's happened now is that our work has entered the public domain and so we can't really stop museums taking an interest in it. It's there, it's history, it's recuperation, it's whatever you like. At the same time, I thought the title of the exhibition was quite nice. I especially liked the subtitle, *About the Situationist International*. And now that I'm getting older and I want to earn a living, it's nice to see this work doing something for me after all these years.

Home: I notice there's been little support for the show from Bernstein or Debord.

Rumney: There wouldn't be. Michele Bernstein, because she doesn't need it. It's pointless to her, it's something she did and from which she now more or less dissociates herself. Not that she's ashamed of it, or disagrees with it, but because she's doing other things and that's it. Debord just has to keep up this view of himself as being totally intransigent.

Home: Whereas the Scandinavians, the Situationist Bauhaus and Group Spur would seem more supportive of the exhibition.

Rumney: They all turned up at the private view and were

doing little happenings, which I rather disapproved of. I went to the opening to see the exhibition and because I wanted to meet old friends and learn a few things. There's a lot of work in the show which I'd not seen before.

Home: I think the exhibition is going to surprise a lot of people in London. Situationist theory is considered relatively sophisticated, whereas most of the painting is extremely primitive.

Rumney: Gallizio was a total primitive. Jorn was not an unsophisticated painter but he created the Institute for Comparative Vandalism; he was an intellectual primitive. Primitivism had a very strong influence on COBRA and also on the Germans. I don't know if I'm wrong to make this distinction but I think of myself as a completely different kind of painter. I could never have joined COBRA.

Home: But it's this type of painting which dominates the exhibition.

Rumney: Yes, it does, it's very strong painting. The curators asked me to lend paintings and I said no, my paintings aren't anything to do with it. I would have been inclined to lend some of the erotic things, but the dates are wrong.

Home: These are the polaroids and plaster casts that you exhibited at Transmission Gallery in 1985 and which were also included in your recent retrospective at England & Co.

Rumney: Which I regard as more situationist, more political, than most of my other work.

Home: To return to the Situationist exhibition, how do you see the public reacting to it?

Rumney: I read the visitors book and that was very interesting. Almost everyone who'd written in it had said this is disgraceful, situationists in a museum, what a load of rubbish! I, however, believe that history should be recorded. I have also come to believe in museums. One of their functions is to make ideas available to people. When we were making our work, the last place we wanted to find it was in a museum. But it's all over now, and I don't see why it shouldn't be recorded, catalogued, documented and so on.

Home: One of the good things about the exhibition is to demonstrate that there's post–war work which stands up alongside the achievements of the futurists, dadaists and surrealists. It's as strong as anything they did. What are your feelings about this?

Rumney: My feelings are somewhat mixed because I regard my painting as very much distinct from Nordic, COBRA-based, Expressionist works. I don't like this type of painting very much. I liked Asger Jorn's work, it's extremely distinguished. I liked Gallizio as a person but I'm not crazy about his work.

Home: I thought his Anti–Material Cave was the strongest thing in the show.

Rumney: Of course it was, it's amazing. There's this primitive reality about Gallizio. I think the splits within the movement were due to it containing both intellectuals and these rather marvellous primitives. I'm not convinced that the intellectuals necessarily made the greatest contribution to the group. It was what was actually done that was important, far more important than the theory. Theories are evanescent. Situationist theory was intentionally inspissated, to make it difficult to understand and extremely difficult to criticise.

Home: And also to give an impression of complete originality! But what about influences?

Rumney: The College Of Pataphysics was an influence on the Situationists. Debord hated anything which could be seen as having influenced him. He saw the College Of Pataphysics as a wretched little coterie. I declined to become a member of the College because of the Situationists. I liked their publications, they had a coherence and a persistent line of thought running through them which if you look at the twelve issues of Internationale Situationiste, is not there. Now then, that may actually be in favour of the IS and say something rather good about it, because where I would criticise Debord is that he wanted to be in charge of the group, he wanted to set up a party line and he wanted everyone to toe it. In fact he never really achieved this and consequently you get this amalgam of divergent ideas which did amalgamate in the first three days of May '68, and in the punk movement. It's not every little group of twelve that can lay claim, thirty years later, to having had any influence on two events as important as that.

Home: To return to Debord, what I find interesting about him is this sense that he always needs a collaborator, whether it be Wolman, Jorn, Vaneigem or Sanguinetti.

Rumney: Sanguinetti is where he met his match. He got a collaborator who was smarter than he was. Sanguinetti is absolutely brilliant.

Home: There's a figure who I feel is always lurking in the background of the situationist saga, and that's Michele Bernstein. I get this feeling that she played a key role within the movement, but I can't specify exactly what it was she contributed.

Rumney: You can't put your finger on it because she won't tell you and she wouldn't thank me if I told you. Since she was my wife, I've got to respect her wishes. I can tell you various little things. She typed all the Potlatchs, all the IS journals and so on. One of the curious things about the IS was that it was extraordinarily anti-feminist in its practice. Women were there to type, cook supper and so on. I rather disapproved of this. Michele had, and has, an extraordinarily powerful and perceptive mind which is shown by the fact that she is among the most important literary critics in France today. A lot of the theory, particularly the political theory, I think originated with Michele rather than Debord, he just took it over and put his name to it.

Home: Something I found strange about the exhibition was that there was no real acknowledgement of influences. There was very little about the Lettristes or the International Movement For An Imaginist Bauhaus.

Rumney: That's the fault of the curators. They might have found it very difficult to do in any other way.

Home: The presentation of the exhibition is very low-tech, the books are displayed on weathered boards, how do you feel about this?

Rumney: I don't feel anything one way or another; they can present it how they like. It's their exhibition. It's not my exhibition, it's the curators, Beaubourg, they've done the exhibition. Apparently there was a vast shortage of money for the show. On the one hand, Beaubourg's been crying out about this. On the other hand, they're apparently charging the ICA an absolute fortune to have it. It seems extremely odd that they didn't have enough money to do a little bit more. I think the curating was wrong because whatever one says or feels about Isou, it should have started with him. That would have made the historical exhibition I'd have liked to see. I feel that the Situationists have somehow achieved this trick of commandeering and imposing a version of history, rather than allowing it to be told as it was.

Home: I found the inclusion of Art and Language and NATO rather mystifying.

Rumney: That's the curators, Peter Wollen and Mark Francis. I met them both and neither of them struck me as serious experts. They were asking questions about things I'd expect them to know. The English tend to be a bit soft intellectually. You could say they are supermarket intellectuals; anything that'll go in the trolley, let's have it.

First published in *Art Monthly,* June 1989

Captive of the KLF

Several of the journalists who were invited to a recent demonstration of 'sonic weapons' by former KLF star Jimmy Cauty have described the event as a fiasco. I was among the cynical stringers who were promised a helicopter trip to Dartmoor, but ended up stranded at Exeter airport after fog swept over the test site and the pilot refused to land.

Eventually, a fleet of taxis transported us to a pub in Ashburton, where one at a time we were allowed to talk with Cauty. I bagged the last interview. Instead of looking like the dejected host of a public relations disaster, with the invited audience missing the event, the smile on Cauty's face gave the impression he'd just pulled off the greatest triumph of his career.

After ten minutes of banal conversation, I confronted Jimmy with the accusation that his recent activities had been financed from the proceeds of record bootlegging. Cauty shrugged his shoulders and laughed. I named a couple of Charles Manson CDs which it is alleged had helped finance his art terrorism. "I could just deny it," Jimmy said laconically, "but those releases are semi-legit. With Manson banged up and no publishing deal on the songs, there's no way anyone can enforce copyright on that stuff. You could drive a tank through the legal loopholes on the Manson material. Besides, I've done far worse things than exploit unenforceable copyrights! Come on, I'll show you."

Cauty led me to a jeep, where I was blindfolded by an assistant who was introduced as Gimpo. After a long and bumpy ride, I was guided across a gravel drive, then down a series of steps into an underground warehouse. Once my blindfold had been removed, I was greeted by Cauty's KLF partner Bill Drummond. Clad in a blood-stained butcher's apron, Drummond was dragging a garden roller through a maze of shelves. I learnt later that Bill was planning to go out to make a few crop circles. I blinked under the bright fluorescent strip lights, feeling decidedly queasy as I took in the carcass of a freshly slaughtered cow. Behind the dead heifer were banks of shelves and innumerable crates, which were stacked right up to the ceiling.

"Those are first generation copies of banned video nasties." Drummond said as he followed my gaze. "We could be fined £20,000 for each tape. Whatever you're into, we've got it."

Cauty led me past racks of CDs and vinyl albums. Not all of these were bootlegs, at least not technically, since much of the stock was by the KLF. Alongside Manson CDs, there was also a wide selection of material by the likes of Prince and Morrissey. At the back of the warehouse was Jimmy's pride and joy, his arsenal of weapons. These included bazookas, grenade launchers, mortars, bombs, airburst mines, flame throwers and plenty of other stuff that I couldn't identify.

"The show I put on tonight," Cauty explained, referring to the demonstration of his sonic weapons, "was a diversion. Moving our base of operations to the West Country has been a logistical nightmare, particularly since the entertainment industry has had us under surveillance for several years. At first, operating as the KLF provided good cover for our bootlegging activities. However, by the time we won the Brit Awards, the KLF had become a millstone around our necks. We were always being shadowed by the press, which impeded the dodgier end of our business dealings. Tonight, we finally succeeded in moving five tons of bootlegs out of a London warehouse without being molested by the copyright enforcement squad."

"That's right," Bill drawled as he joined us, "we've always had the last laugh in our dealings with the music industry. One time we were passed a million quid in marked notes as part of a sting operation. We could have just dumped the hot cash, but instead we burnt it and declared the ashes to be art. That really annoyed the cartel of multinationals who were desperate to prove we'd been pirating their acts."

"People view us as eccentric," Cauty elaborated, "but cultivating a wacky imagine is good for business. You only have to look at Howard Hughes to see that. We make and lose more money in any given year than the average family sees over several generations. The important thing is ensuring that our assets are properly liquefied. We can make a fortune just switching our money between currencies. Personally, I'm seriously addicted to the futures market. It's a real thrill being able to buy things that don't exist!"

"The money doesn't mean that much to us," Drummond added hastily, "it's just a marker of our success. However, as far as I'm concerned, music was never enough. Someone once said that crime is the highest form of sensuality but I think that's rubbish, since the biggest criminals are the heads of multinational corporations. I see myself as a modern day Robin Hood. I make sure that ten per cent of the profits from my bootlegs is ploughed back into worthwhile causes."

"That's all very well," I observed, "but why the hell are you telling me all this?"

"Why not tell you?" Jimmy shot back. "No one is going to believe it. We're going to blindfold you when you leave, you'll never be able to find this place again. I don't care what you write. You can make it all up if you like. You can even quote me as saying that."

First published in *The Big Issue 195,* 19–25 August 1996

ROYAL WATCH:
THE IMAGE HAS CRACKED

IT COMES AS NO SURPRISE that the revelations made in previous *Royal Watch* columns have been met with complete silence from the mainstream British media. Establishment figures know that I have written the truth and realise that if they attack my research, this will simply serve to draw attention to it. In underground circles, individuals in the pay of the Crown, as well as those who are simply thick, have been heard to assert that what I write is just a joke, that it is humour with no factual basis. These attempts to discredit me will very shortly backfire on the idiots who have perpetrated them.

Even those who have failed to take my warnings seriously will recall that, in the first *Royal Watch* column, I revealed the monarchy was involved in illicit drug running operations. No one denies that the British establishment played a major role in the opium trade of the last century, but many otherwise open-minded individuals refuse to believe that such activities are still a major source of income for the monarchy in the nineteen-nineties. Now the mask has slipped, a front page headline in *The Sunday Times* of 20 November 1994 screamed *British Envoys Buy Heroin To Lure Top Dealers*. Although justifying these activities with the lie that they are a form of detective work, enabling investigators to test how drug trafficking networks operate, the story confirmed that "British diplomats are procuring millions of pounds worth of heroin from illegal factories in Pakistan."

It is now officially admitted that drugs are stored in embassies and diplomatic offices "before being flown to Britain on scheduled passenger flights." These "covert imports are disclosed in correspondence between diplomats at the British high commission in Islamabad and the director of intelligence of the Pakistan Narcotics Control Board." The *Sunday Times* story then goes on to give details of a specific shipment of heroin that was couriered to Manchester by a Crown official. It is, therefore, hardly surprising that the royal family goes to such lengths to disguise the extent of its wealth, since much of its money comes from a long term and ongoing involvement in the narcotics trade!

Members of the royal family enjoy the adulation their position brings, but this visibility is also useful in diverting attention away from the real purpose of their global tours, which is to broker drug deals and indulge their taste in ritual human sacrifice! However, in recent years the credibility of the monarchy has been undermined by rifts between the Queen and her children, which led to various royal scandals being aired in public. The Queen knows that Prince Charles has been plotting to have her ritually sacrificed in 1997, and as a consequence, she has been fighting back tooth and claw. Charles has been thrown to the dogs and the press can write whatever they like about him, while mention of the Queen's extramarital love affairs remains strictly taboo.

A headline in the *Times* of 3 November 1994 revealed that *Royal Scandals Raise Support For Australian Republicans*. This story gave the impression that it was Charles and Diana's extramarital activities that had fuelled republicanism in the antipodes. In fact, it is the knowledge that the entire royal family is swirling in a cesspool of filth which has turned the sensible Aussies against the House of Windsor. Earlier this summer, under the headline *Banned In Britain*, Australia's biggest selling weekly magazine, *Woman's Day*, serialised parts of *Queen Elizabeth II: A Woman Who Is Not Amused*. *Woman's Day* summarised the state of royal play with the following sentence: "Philip's many affairs drove Elizabeth to find solace elsewhere as Nicholas Davies reveals in his sensational new book, in which he also tells of Diana's indiscretions and Anne's love child."

The Queen's most significant affair, since it also entailed a huge amount of sex magick, was with Henry George Reginald Molyneux Herbert, seventh Earl of Carnarvon. The Earl's grandfather had discovered the tomb of Tutankhamen after being initiated into a top occult order. Mystic secrets had been passed down through the family, and Lizzie figured that a fling with the Earl, called 'Porchy' by his mistress, was the easiest way of gaining his confidence and simultaneously expanding her esoteric knowledge. The only other man with whom the Queen is definitely known to have engaged in sex magick is Patrick Terence William Span, seventh Baron Plunkett, although there are indications that Sir John Miller may have played a supporting role in several of Lizzie's rites of Satanic perversion. Clearly, the Crown is in serious trouble, and if Lizzie's affairs are widely publicised in Britain, it is finished. Spread the word: their kingdom will fall!

First published in *Underground 5,* Winter 1994

HOXTON SUBLIME: THE WORK OF LOTTE GLOB

FASCINATED BY THE CERAMIC FOUNTAIN visible through the locked gates of Hackney Community College on Hoxton Street, I decided to track down Lotte Glob, the artist who created it. A phone call resulted in an invitation to the artist's studio at Balnakeil, a former MOD early warning station on the north coast of Scotland that has been transformed into a craft village. To get there I flew to Inverness, then took a train to Lairg. I'd missed the once-a-day post-bus to the north coast of Sutherland, so Glob made the hundred and twenty mile round trip to pick me up in her van. The brooding mountains and winding single track road made me nervous about Lotte's foot-to-the-floor night driving. She reassured me that she'd been living at Balnakeil for thirty years and knew every twist and turn in our route.

When we reached Lotte's home my eyes were dazzled by the reflection of the headlights on the bright figurative ceramic designs that decorated its outer walls. The pine interior was a classic example of Scandinavian functionalism. Lotte is the daughter of P.V. Glob, the Danish archaeologist whose book *The Bog People* has been translated into dozens of languages. Despite her Scandinavian background, Lotte's hospitality turned out to be archetypally Scottish. As soon as I sat down she poured me a large malt whisky. The rich cultural mix that has fed into Glob's work gives it a vibrancy and variety that's rarely encountered in the work of potters based in the British Isles. The use of bright colours in certain pieces illustrates the influence of the Scandinavian avant-garde, and in particular painters such as

Asger Jorn who was a founder member of both COBRA and the Situationist International. However, as I was to discover the next day, local scenery and culture are also a big influence.

For a decade Glob has been making ceramics that she places on remote windswept mountains in the area surrounding Cape Wrath. These pieces are fabricated from materials collected around Balnakeil such as pebbles, seaweed and fungi. Arranged in clay these natural objects are fired to white heat so that they meld together. Their flowing forms recall the volcanic origins of the Highland landscape. Known collectively as The Ultimate Rock Garden, viewing these works can be an arduous task. To see just one piece, I was driven out to Loch Eriboll. From the roadside, it was a hard two hour slog up the side of a burn and over a couple of hills before I got to see a work that had been sited in the wilds. For someone in her early fifties, Lotte is extremely fit. I was knackered from our climb but Glob looked like she'd done no more than take a stroll down a garden path. She told me I'd seen one of the more accessible pieces. Fortunately, photographs and field notes enable those not willing to spend hours trekking over hills to get some idea of what the work is about.

While I was out with Glob, I noticed that she was collecting animal bones as well as stones, plants and pieces of wood, all of which were stuffed into a rucksack. These would be used in future works. When we got back to Lotte's studio she showed me some collaborative pieces she was creating with the Dundee based multi-media artist Marshall Anderson. Produced under the name Anderson Glob these included a series of ceramic books made from animal bones, rock, sediments and peat that had been combined with paper, wax, photographs and drawings. Visual puns such as the use of animal spines to create the spines of various books were obviously designed to bring into question the status of mass-produced cultural objects. Each animal book used the bones of a single species. The rabbit and fox books were fairly easy to handle but the cheviot book made from the bones of several sheep was massive.

Glob had also developed a way of treating ordinary books so that she could fire them in her kiln. Likewise, she'd found a way of transforming peat into black paper, and from sheets of this material Anderson was stitching together small blank pads that were far too fragile to write on. The Anderson Glob books were to be viewed and admired but could not be read as pieces of written language or, indeed, as any form of conventional narrative. Instead, they can be seen as avatars of the future or else fossils left behind in the wake of electronic publishing. Anderson and Glob were unaware of the work of writers such as H. P. Lovecraft but their collaborative efforts struck me as the perfect physical embodiment of forbidden occult books described in horror fiction. The extraordinary form of these works left me feeling that they might contain the 'original' manuscript, describing the death of the universe, said to have been discovered amongst rural Irish ruins in the classic fantasy novel *The House On The Borderland* by William Hope Hodgson.

Lotte Glob's Far North Ceramics studio is surrounded by jagged mountains, rugged coast and surging seas. The weather can change from bright sunshine to a howling gale in the space of a few minutes. The cliffs and mountains are chiselled by year-round storms that gust in from the Arctic circle. The scenery surrounding Glob's workshop is every bit as extraordinary as the landscape described by Hope Hodgson. To one side of this studio is a ceramic fountain identical in design to Glob's work for Hackney Community College. Both incorporate hollow ceramic stones that are driven around a pool of water by a gentle spray. In Hackney some joker placed a yellow plastic duck amongst these stones. I can't imagine that happening at Balnakeil. The Highland landscape in which the fountain outside Glob's studio is set transforms its organic contours into something sublime. In this setting her ceramic works don't look like pretty ornaments, they are awe-inspiring.

Lotte Glob's Far North Ceramics shop is open all day during the tourist season and sells both functional and ornamental objects. Glob's tea pots, in particular, are highly recommended. To reach the shop take the A838 to Durness then follow the signs to Balnakeil Craft Village. Glob's studio and shop are housed in the first building on the left as you enter the village.

An edited version of this text previously appeared in *AN Magazine,* May 1998

BRINGING IT ALL BACK HOME

Stewart Home interviewed by himself.

HAVING EMBARKED on a series of interviews to promote my novel *Come Before Christ And Murder Love* (Serpent's Tail) and the anthology *Mind Invaders: A Reader in Psychic Warfare, Cultural Sabotage and Semiotic Terrorism* (Serpent's Tail), it struck me that I was far better qualified to interview myself than those who were being paid to do the job. Given both this and the fact that *Come Before Christ* features doppelgängers the like of which haven't been seen since E. T. A. Hoffman's *The Devil's Elixirs* was first published in German nearly two hundred years ago, followers of Freud may discern schizophrenic tendencies in my work. However, since I consider the notion of the unconscious to be a nonsense, whatever maladies psychoanalysts claim to divine in my prose are of no concern to me.

Stewart: Do you have a set schedule when you write?
Home: Usually, like when I'm doing a piece of journalism, I'm given a word count and a deadline, then I just scream along as I type and it's done before I know it. Of course, I do get complaints from the neighbours, who sometimes want to know why the hell I'm making so much noise at three in the morning. The phone goes all day, so I prefer to write at night. You know, once you've got a cult reputation people just call with the most ridiculous propositions, like do you want to host a tv show? It never stops. Weekdays 10 am to 6 pm is really bad, so I lounge about in my silk pyjamas munching cashew nuts. Between six and midnight the calls are a mixture of my friends and nutters

wanting to buy rock memorabilia I threw away years ago, not to mention a surprising number of strangers who want to give me blow jobs or have me kick them down the stairs into their basement, and thinking I'll be thrilled that they want to be my slave. So in the evening I answer letters and listen to old soul records. After midnight there aren't so many phone calls, so I slip into my Crazy Gang kit and sit at my desk writing fiction or journalism while knocking back strong coffee and drams of classic malts like Ardbeg, Bruichladdich, Glenfarclas, Glen Scotia, Laphroaig, Macallan, Scapa or Talisker. If the neighbours come up to complain about the noise of me screaming as I type, I usually open the door and holler "Wimbledon! Wimbledon!" while shying salted peanuts at them. Interruptions used to be quite a problem after my last move, but the other people in the block have got used to me now, and once they realised I was a writer I think they were less puzzled by what they viewed as my eccentric behaviour.

Anyway, I just scream through the night, then have a bath at about 7 am and go to bed. I only need three or four hours sleep, so I'm always up well before lunch. What I write varies; I have binges on different forms. The journalism is quickly turned over when it comes in and I have intemperate bouts of book writing. Then I just stick the answerphone on and write eighteen hours a day until the thing is finished. I don't keep a journal but these days I save copies of all the letters I write. Just had my first collection of letters out – it felt like a book without any effort.

Stewart: Do you use note cards, do you carry a notebook or scribble on napkins?

Home: Occasionally I'll take a notebook out when I'm going somewhere and want to describe it. Usually I just use my memory for stuff like that, or I'm checking in books. I don't use note cards or plans, I just get an idea and run it straight onto the computer when I'm doing a book. Of course, I'm reading all the time but I never write in books or make notes, I just throw in a scrap of paper to mark the page if I come across something

I think I'll want to go back to. This works fine with books I've acquired permanently as long as I remember not to lend them to other people. It's a bit more of a problem with books I've borrowed from friends or used in the library, it just doesn't seem to work with them; the bits of paper tend to fall out if someone else reads the book.

I also have a great fondness for old envelopes. I tend to write messages all over them. They usually get filled up with people's numbers. I have piles of them by the phone and I can never find the numbers I want because I've written all over the back and front of every envelope and there are usually dozens of them lying around. As a result I'm pretty bad at returning calls because generally I can't find anyone's phone number, and there comes a point where I get so fed up with all the scribbled over envelopes lying around that I just throw them away. Then I leave a message on my answermachine saying I've lost my address book and can everyone who calls leave their number. But I don't use these envelopes for my writing, they aren't an alternative to using a notebook. I just prefer the spontaneity of jumping right into writing – preparation is for wimps.

Stewart: Do you think of yourself as an underground writer?

Home: Not really, I tend to think of people like Burroughs and Ginsberg as being underground, six feet underground to be precise. In fact I try to avoid the underground, especially in the summer and during the rush hour when it gets unpleasantly hot in the tube trains. I prefer the buses. I'm particularly fond of the S2 route that goes from Stratford to Clapton Pond. It's well cool, especially the bit where it loops down from the Bow Flyover to Bromley-by-Bow. I'm also well into the portion of the 35 route between London Bridge and Clapham, particularly the bit where you go through the Elephant and Castle. In London, there was a time when they were putting poems next to the advertising in the subway trains, but it was always really naff. I wouldn't want my poems put up on underground trains, I'd prefer to see them on the side of a 22 bus.

Stewart: Who do you admire?

Home: A Catalonian monk called Raymond Lull who lived in the fourteenth century. He was a logician and invented, amongst other things, the *Ars Magna*. This is a universal system of true statements derived by the means of tables which can be combined in mechanical ways. The result is a machine which creates philosophical questions about and reflections on universal truth. Lull actually created this machine as a tool to convert non–Christians. The tables and the ideas it used were based on what Lull believed would be accepted as true in all religions. So he used this combinatory table for converting non-Christians to Christianity. Obviously, it is secular appropriations of Lull rather than Lull himself that interest me. These really began to gain ground with Athanasius Kircher in the seventeenth century. Kircher was a Jesuit and wrote, among many other books, a new *Ars Combinatoria* which paved the way for practical applications of Lullism such as algorithmic permutation in poetry, especially in the speculative poetic plays of Harsdörffer, Kuhlmann and others.

Stewart: What inspires you to write?

Home: A mixture of things, like I might look at my bank account and realise I'm running out of money, so I'll knock up a novel to get an advance on it. You know, or I might hear a bit of conversation, something like "you want to split up and I want to split up, that means we've got something in common." I heard that and had to write a novel I could put it in. However, I don't really need to be inspired to write, I'm more or less addicted to it. Especially when I'm writing some kind of social critical piece, I just get into it and see where an argument takes me. It can be surprising – I end up with opinions that ten years before I couldn't have imagined holding. Working through arguments is the best kind of magickal mystery tour, you go down roads you've never been down before, so you really haven't got a clue where you're gonna end up.

Stewart: How would you like to be remembered?

Home: I won't be remembered; as my writing becomes increasingly self-referential, I am rendered invisible. It is not so much a case of me wanting to be invisible, I am being rendered invisible whether I want this or not. Invisibility is an inevitable by-product of fame, the concrete individual is lost amid a plethora of hype, the image of the star is shaped by the fantasies and dreams of those who idolise them. The multiple identity is a way of publicly laying bare dreams of both invisibility and fame. This is one of the reasons I got involved in these projects where a lot of people were writing under the same name. When you have an open situation with a number of people using the same name and sharing an identity, you have an extreme case of an arbitrary signifier because there is no pretence that the name is unique in the way that someone might think the words Paul Smith refer to one individual. In fact, Paul Smith isn't a unique signifier. When I saw Wire playing on the South Bank a year ago, a middle-aged woman asked me how I'd got in to what was basically a private party. I told her that I knew Paul Smith and she thought I was talking about the clothes designer rather than the bloke who runs Blast First Records and had organised the Wire gig.

With a shared name and identity like Luther Blissett or Karen Eliot, which are names various people have been involved in using collectively, the name is fixed, but the people using it aren't. From one perspective, the use of a multiple name is extremely arbitrary. You have an extremely flexible signifier and signified relationship. There is no fixed referent, merely a fiction created by those using the name. However, as soon as you use a multiple name, by sharing the identity and adopting an arbitrary signifier, you immediately find that you are in a position to mould both the signifier and what is signified. Suddenly you find yourself involved in something that is a perfect example of what a cabbalist might call Edenic language. By doing something as Luther Blissett, you find yourself actively shaping this identity. The relationship between the signified and signifier no longer appears arbitrary because each is shaped and mediated by the other. It follows that multiple names create a flip-flop effect in which those using them unlock the secrets of infinity.

A slightly truncated version of this piece previously appeared in *Sick Again!* Spring 98 under the title 'Rotten, Boring And Imbecilic: Stewart Home interviewed by himself'.

SWAP-SHOP ARTISTS

ANYONE SERIOUS about joining the haute-bourgeoisie wants to fill their home with original works of art. However, this can prove expensive, and I've long been looking for a way of investing in art without bankrupting myself. So you can imagine my excitement when I heard that an arts local exchange trading scheme (LETS) was being set up in Hackney.

LETS enables people to trade goods and services without any money changing hands. Instead, it's possible to run up interest free debts by offering payment in kind to other members of the scheme. Since many different people are involved in each local group, all sorts of services are on offer. Central records are kept, so it's possible to earn LETS doing child-minding for someone who offers aromatherapy, and to then spend them with a third party who does carpet cleaning.

Although I hadn't been very impressed by the organic vegetables a friend traded for piano lessons on a rural LETS scheme, Hackney Art LETS sounded more promising. I had visions of filling my flat with huge canvases in return for plugging struggling artists in *The Big Issue*. With this end in mind, I visited Art LETS facilitator Les Moore at his Hackney Wholefoods store. Les was a no-nonsense Yorkshire-man, and I was worried he might think the service I was offering other Hackney Art LETS members sounded flaky.

"You're the first person to offer fifteen minutes of fame in exchange for art pounds," Les beamed.

"What are the other members doing?" I enquired.

"Several people who have vans are offering a specialist art transport service, to get pieces to and from exhibitions."

"That's not the sort of thing I'm looking for, I want to acquire original works of art on your LETS scheme."

"I'm not encouraging that sort of thing," Les said sternly. "LETS is designed to work in parallel with the existing monetary system, stimulating the local economy and enabling people to enjoy services they couldn't otherwise afford. I don't think people should sell art works on LETS. Pricing art on LETS would create too many problems. We do, however, have someone who does batik work that will knock your socks off!"

Since I detest hippie gear, I wracked my brains trying to think of something I'd want to buy with 'art pounds'. Eventually, I asked Les if he had someone who could forge signatures. The disapproving look I got led me to hastily explain that the pop artist Andy Warhol used to boast he would sign anything. When I met Warhol in the mid-eighties, I'd tested this claim by asking him to sign a copy of the *SCUM Manifesto* by Valerie Solanas, the radical feminist who'd shot and seriously injured him in the late sixties. Somewhat predictably, Warhol refused to sign my book. Now that Warhol was dead, a copy of the *SCUM Manifesto* with 'his' signature on the fly-leaf would provide a nice 'momento' of this encounter.

Les was horrified by the idea: "LETS has an important role to play in local communities, I couldn't possibly allow it to be associated with fraud!"

I tried telling Les about recent trends in art. After all, Warhol had paid people to make art works that he simply signed, and he'd even sent off a double to do a lecture tour. Les wasn't convinced by my arguments and I was fast losing interest in his group. My growing suspicions that his scheme was unlikely to attract the type of 'con artist' I admire was confirmed when Maria Pinschof joined us.

"A lot of artists feel isolated," Maria explained, "and so something I will be offering on LETS is critical assessment of work. Galleries do no more than tell you what they like. To have another artist look critically at what you do, and make suggestions about how you might progress, is something a lot of people want and Hackney Art LETS will provide it."

Maria's self-assured manner satisfied me she'd provide excellent advice to anyone concerned about their artistic development. However, since I was after big canvases on the never-never, Maria's spiel also convinced me Hackney Art LETS wasn't my bag. I wasn't interested in 'personal growth', I wanted Damien Hirst cutting my hair and David Hockney in to do the plumbing. The last thing I need is someone to tell me my writing is littered with clichés. I already have a grammar analyser on my computer that does this with such frequency that I no longer use it.

At the end of the day, Hackney Art LETS has more to do with fostering 'community spirit' than providing arts professionals with the services they require. Les Moore accepts LETS as part payment on goods at his health food store, but I shop at Kwik Save. Likewise, you can forget about David Hockney doing your plumbing; I think you'd be very lucky to find a qualified plumber in any LETS group. The LETS movement is top heavy with people offering 'rebirthing', while electricians and gas fitters are in short supply. Thus, Hackney Art LETS appears fated to attract people with a 'new age' outlook, while simultaneously repelling anyone cynical enough to make it in the art world.

First published in *The Big Issue 201*,
30 September-6 October 1996

MARLBOROUGH MAZE

AMIDST THE RECENT HYPE surrounding young British art, the pundits promoting this scam overlooked a number of cultural forms that might have provided a more solid platform from which to promote their rather dubious agenda. Early in 1997 the Norton Museum of Art in Florida hosted a major exhibition entitled *An Amazing Art: Contemporary Labyrinths by Adrian Fisher*. Portsmouth based Fisher has been designing labyrinths for donkey's years and played a major role in organising *The Year of the Maze* in 1991, a celebration of the 300th anniversary of Hampton Court, the oldest surviving hedge maze in England.

Many new mazes were built as part of the 1991 celebrations, and Fisher bagged the prime spot at Blenheim Palace, Oxfordshire. Blenheim occupies the site of the legendary Rosamund's Bower, an architectural labyrinth with heavy defences in which Henry II is said to have installed his mistress Fair Rosamund. According to the story propagated by various popular ballads, when Queen Eleanor finally penetrated the maze in 1176, she forced her rival to drink poison. Blenheim Palace replaced the ruined medieval buildings in the eighteenth century and was given to the First Duke of Marlborough in recognition of his many military victories. The Marlborough family's other famous military scion, Winston Churchill, was born at Blenheim in 1874.

Fisher based his Marlborough Maze design on Grinling Gibbons' Blenheim Palace roof carvings depicting the Panoply of Victory. Seen from above, the lines of yew hedges that make up the labyrinth portray pyramids of cannonballs, a cannon firing, and the air filled with banners, flags and bugles.

The maze has entrances on the left and right with a central exit. Two wooden bridges add an exciting additional aspect to the puzzle element of the maze, while simultaneously providing viewing points from which to survey the work. One of Fisher's colour mazes can also be found at Blenheim. This labyrinth consists of nodes connected by coloured paths, the choice of path at each node being determined by the colour of the path previously taken.

Mums and dads stop on the bridges of the main maze to view a piece of symbolism that makes Sarah Lucas look subtle. Children race around the labyrinth enjoying the three-dimensionality of the work in the same way that they might relish Tracy Emin's *Everyone I Ever Slept With* tent. The Marlborough Maze isn't difficult to solve – the first time I went in it took about twelve minutes to get out again. Alongside the aesthetic frisson of the mock pompous symbolism, the twists and turns of the labyrinth cause the maze to echo with the noise of laughter and wonderment. The crowds flocking to Blenheim are very different to the audience attracted by young British art. On the surface those using the labyrinth may appear less sophisticated than gallery groupies, but beneath this superficial appearance their aesthetic tastes are actually far more radical.

The institutional defeat of modernism has resulted in an increasing assimilation of art into the representational categories of popular culture. The Marlborough Maze is a perfect example of an art that does not have to justify such pleasures to its audience. This has generated a certain amount of confusion in the interpretation of Fisher's work, and while his mazes have received coverage everywhere from *Scientific American* to *Der Speigal*, they are largely ignored by the art press. Art critics generally view Fisher as politically conformist, intellectually timid and an aesthetic revisionist. Such views are extremely parochial since they are based on the surface appearances of Fisher's work at the expense of the wider cultural context.

While young British art has been justified as a demotically

voiced assault on politically correct post-modernism, the Marlborough Maze attacks something infinitely more sacrosanct. Woodstock Park in which Blenheim Palace is situated was landscaped by Capability Brown, whose naturalistic aesthetic resulted in the destruction of many mazes and the formal gardens of which they constituted a part. Hampton Court Maze only survives today because Brown was told not to touch it. This must have irritated the Royal Gardener, since he lived in the house next to the maze for twenty years!

The Marlborough Maze is much more than merely a slap in the face for aesthetically 'educated' taste or a simple parody that sets ghosts walking. Despite Fisher's unqualified regard for the voluptuous pleasures of popular culture, he does not seek to assimilate himself to popular culture in fazed admiration, as if his only ambition was an anti-intellectual release of libidinal energy. Rather, he treats the aesthetically despised pleasures of maze-making and walking as something that is first nature and commonplace and mutually defining of subjectivity. The labyrinth is a vibrant cultural form precisely because it has avoided the aesthetic hype of the contemporary art market. As such, Fisher and maze-walking represent the future direction of visual culture.

Previously published in *Variant*
Vol 2 no 5, Spring 1998

"STREET FICTIONS"

ALTHOUGH I'M SPEAKING at this Street Fictions conference I want to make it clear from the outset that I disagree with the premises that have been used to promote it. I do not consider my novels to exhibit a 'new streetwise toughness' or claim to be alert to 'the brash realities of the street'. Rather, I consider the contention that 'the street' provides access to experiences that are somehow 'authentic' and 'unmediated' as being always and already a literary construction. While it strikes me as being little more than an ill-considered marketing exercise, I've found my writing labelled as both 'transgressive fiction' and 'street fiction'. I find this slippage between 'transgressive' and 'street' suggestive, since both labels serve to foster the illusion that, not only was there once a common and dominant literary culture that shaped and moulded all forms of writing but, this fictive canon still exists. I will return to the subject of 'street fiction' presently, but first a 'digression'.

While the works of Raymond Williams are curiously lopsided, this does not render them utterly useless.[1] In *The Country And The City* (Paladin, St Albans 1975, p. 351), Williams observes:

> Looking back, for example, on the English history, and especially on its culmination in imperialism, I can see in this process of the altering relations of country and city the driving force of a mode of production which has indeed transformed the world. I am then very willing to see the city as capitalism, as so many now do, if I can say also that this mode of production began, specifically, in the English rural economy, and produced,

there, many of the characteristic effects – increases of production, physical rendering of a totally available world, displacement of customary settlements, a human remnant and force which became a proletariat – which have since been seen, in many extending forms, in cities and colonies and in an international system as a whole. It then does not surprise me that the complaints in Covent Garden echo the complaints of the commoners, since the forces of improvement and development, in those specific forms – an amalgam of financial and political power which is pursuing different ends from those of any local community but which has its own and specific internal rationale – are in a fundamental sense similar, as phases of capitalist enterprise.

In his book, Williams teases out both pastoral and urban literary traditions, which are mediated not only by the preceding writing in each category, but also by each other. More recently, Jonathan Rutherford in *Forever England: Reflections On Masculinity And Empire* (Lawrence & Wishart, London 1997, p. 51) discusses the "predominance of pastoral images in discourses of Englishness" and links this to the ruthless urbanisation as a source of British wealth. While Rutherford is often suggestive, he over emphasises the importance of writers such as G. K. Chesterton, Hillaire Belloc, E. M. Forster, A. E. Houseman, D. H. Lawrence, Thomas Hardy, Edward Thomas, Rupert Brooke and Walter de la Mare. Rutherford talks about the Edwardians rediscovering rural England as a symbol of the country's unchanging essence, but in stressing the green rolling hills and hedgerows of Kent, Sussex and Surrey, his emphasis is misplaced. This landscape might have been and was found anywhere – for example in Constable's paintings of 'Suffolk' or Hardy's 'Wessex' – because it is a simulacrum. There is no England in which pastoral discourse can be grounded because England does not exist.

As Williams illustrates, pastoral discourse can easily be inverted producing the usual gamut of 'metropolitan' clichés about 'rural idiocy'. However, while the industrialisation of the English countryside preceded and made possible urban industrialisation, the ongoing growth of the service sector of the economy in towns has resulted in urban de-industrialisation. While Williams wished to maintain that images of the countryside and the city are mediated and interpenetrated by each other – making it quite impossible to understand either in isolation, once these categories are rendered meaningless there is nothing left to understand. Rather than reversing perspectives, factory farming and urban regeneration are an implosion in which pastoral representations have been engulfed by a simulacrum. The factor that is being addressed here is suburbanisation. Vikki Rix provides one example of these trends in 'Social and Demographic Change In East London':[2]

Population loss took place in all East London boroughs apart from Tower Hamlets, throughout the 1980s. Where have the East London residents moved to? The more affluent white working class, able to enter the owner occupied sector, have moved out of East London areas and settled in many neighbouring Essex boroughs, such as Brentwood, Chelmsford, Epping Forest, Thurrock and Basildon. Cockney Essex as Hobbs argues, is living proof of this out-migration which has largely occurred because of a search for a better quality of life, the greener Essex suburbs being perceived as more attractive localities because of less [sic] population density and more open space. Essex's population density in 1991 was a mere 4.2 compared with London's and Inner London's density of 42.3 and 78.1 respectively. The fact that Essex remains overwhelmingly white and British-born has and continues to be another reason for the out-migration of the white working class of East London; for example 97 per cent of all those residents who moved into Essex boroughs in 1990 were white. As a result of out-migration, Essex gained around 145,000 new residents between 1981 and 1991, a population increase of 10 per cent.

To better understand these demographic shifts, it is useful to compare Rix's survey with Tim Butler's ' "People Like Us": The Gentrification of Hackney in the 1980s':[3]

> The most dramatic change that took place between 1971 and 1991 was the loss of population, which declined by 57,000 or 26 per cent, most of this took place between 1971 and 1981. There is nothing particularly unique to Hackney here; all inner London boroughs lost population during this decade mainly to the outer London boroughs and the rest of the south east... However, within the context of an overall loss of population, the occupational structure of Hackney changed significantly over these years... Broadly... the middle-class group (i.e. professionals, employers and managers) doubled in size between 1971 and 1991. The pattern of this growth is quite complex in that it occurred within the context of a steep decline in both the overall population and in the economically active population. Thus between 1971 and 1981 the actual number of economically active middle-class remained more or less stable although it increased its 'share' of the economically active population (from 7.2 per cent to 9.5 per cent). In the period 1981-91 however, it doubled in size (from 8,198 to 15,220) and constituted nearly 23 per cent of the borough's economically active population. It is this population loss that provides the basis for the gentrification of Hackney in the 1980s. In the 1980s, however, the overall population loss slowed (although the number of economically active people continued to decline significantly) but the actual number of middle class more or less doubled thus increasing their visibility considerably.

Responses to suburbanisation are often emotive, as can be illustrated by way of reference to a book such as *Suburbia* by David Thorns (Paladin, St Albans 1972, p. 11-12):

The most characteristic feature of present-day urbanism in most of the advanced industrial nations, unlike the past, is that of city dispersion, of the outward movement of the population from the city to the surrounding area. The people move out to the suburb, to the land of the semi-detached, the new housing estate, the new town, swamp the old rural villages and turn them into dormitories... The trend towards urban dispersal has led to the shift of the ideological controversy from the city-rural conflict to the city-suburban. In order to understand the latter adequately, the former must be considered. The earliest attackers of city and urban life were those who saw the city as the source of all that was evil and corrupting in life as against the rural life which was the repository of all virtue. This position in American writing on urban life is typified by Thomas Jefferson, with his famous view of the city "as pestilential to morals, health and the liberties of man". The virtues of rural life were extolled by the Romantics who desired the 'wilderness', who were opposed to the organized life which was inevitable consequence of urban development...

While Thorns presents himself as an objective sociologist, his talk of people moving out "to the land of the semi-detached... swamp the old rural villages and turn them into dormitories" betrays the dominance of a code that is draining meaning from his rhetoric. Among contemporary English fiction writers the most visible advocate of suburbia is J. G. Ballard. Despite this, Ballard's work is rooted in European modernist traditions of nihilism structured by notions of identity and significance. Ballard sets out to interpret the contemporary according to this code and to foist the categorical imperative of morality and faith, the sublime imperative of meaning, on the social through an apocalyptic aesthetic. By way of contrast, Iain Sinclair in his psychogeograpchial novels accepts everything and redirects it *en bloc* towards the spectacular, without requiring any other code, without requiring any meaning, ultimately without resistance, but making everything slide into an indeterminate sphere of ambiguity.

An attitude of utter indifference is something that Sinclair shares with Andy Warhol.[4] Through the simple expedient of joining together pre-existing phrases, Sinclair avoids taking a position on anything. In an attempt to inject meaning into words that no longer signify anything, certain literary critics have claimed Sinclair's prose is mystical. However, rather than descending into and unfolding the self, Sinclair's work enfolds representation. In *Downriver* and *Radon Daughters,* Sinclair moves from Inner London to suburban Essex, Kent and beyond. In doing this he abandons all topologies that posit the existence of boundaries between the city and the suburbs, the rural and the urban. It is precisely because this leads to London being absorbed in Sinclair's texts, and ultimately disappearing, that literary opinion attempts to conjure the city back by denouncing these books as London novels. Identical erasures take place in a work called *Seaton Point* (Spare Change Press, London 1998, p. 23) produced collectively by seven young writers:[5]

Malcolm wasn't going to find excitement in Redditch. He had to head for the city, the deprived inner-city that he had heard so much about on the news. To Malcolm, this was a semi-mythical place inhabited by people who were not quite the same as him. Somehow they had always seemed a little less than human — the single mothers, drug dealers and drunks who didn't live to the same standards as the decent folk of Redditch... Malcolm found the centre of Hackney disappointingly tidy, nice even, with its old churches and semi-pedestrianised high street, not at all what he was looking for. He noticed a marked difference in the people, however... The older people looked liked they shopped exclusively at Oxfam, while the younger crowd's clothing was largely uniform, the crusties excepted, with baggy jeans and puffy black jackets very much to the fore. The young black women nonetheless possessed a certain style and swagger, and nearly all of them were good looking.

In this passage all the conventional signifiers of inner city decay are accepted at face value and thus drained of meaning. There are, however, writers who wish to deny that appearances function all by themselves based on a necessity far more implacable than arbitrary chains of causes and effects, and Will Self provides just one example. That said, the media profiles generated by this micro-celebrity negate all the claims Self makes within them on behalf of signification. It is not Self's standing as an intellectual but the banality of his pronouncements that results in the masses accepting his empty words with such impeccable indifference. Self's public reception makes him a doppelgänger of the Victorian 'poet and tragedian' William McGonagall, whose works are still very popular. *The Tay Bridge Disaster,* one of McGonagall's best known poems, concludes:

It must have been an awful sight,
To witness in the dusky moonlight,
While the storm fiend did laugh and angry did bray,
Along the Railway Bridge of the Silv'ry Tay.
Oh! ill-fated Bridge of the Silv'ry Tay,
I must now conclude my lay
By telling the world fearlessly, without the least dismay,
That your central girders would not have given way.
At least many sensible men do say,
Had they been supported on each side with buttresses,
At least many sensible men confesses,
For the stronger we our houses do build,
The less chance we have of being killed.

The manner in which McGonagall anticipated his own destiny is evident in the 'Tribute From Three Students At Glasgow University' incorporated into his *Poetic Gems*. The 'tribute' concludes with a series of questions directed at the author, such as: "Is the most intellectual benefit to be derived from a study of the McGonagallian or Shakespearian school of poetry?" An identical movement beyond description and analysis is evident in 'Arrogant As Usual: Will Self in New York City' by Alexander Laurence in *Cups 86* (New York December 1997). Even more than the title, the photographic captions capture the tone of adulation evident in this piece; they are "Give us that serious author look. Okay great!" and "Will Self takes his hat off for us in Union Square!"

European reviewers tend to be even more reverential to literary giants like Self than their American counterparts. A typical example is 'Good Will Hunting' by Andrew Davies in *The Big Issue 280* (10-26 April 1998, p. 29). Here Self opines: "I attempted to outflank the media by being essentially more intellectual." Only Will Self would consider being more intellectual than the media a challenge; for the masses this outflanking consists of their silence, their capacity to absorb and neutralise. It is a specific internal strength whose effectivity differs from all schemas of production, radiation and expansion according to which the imaginary functions, even in its wish to destroy those schemas. In the same interview, Self treats his use of heroin as if it were further evidence of his oft-repeated claim that he is an intellectual:

> It's a perversion, a psychosexual perversion, but I don't regret it, or all I would be able to write about would be Malcolm Bradbury-style campus books because that's all my experience would have been... I am incredibly bourgeois. I shop at Sainsbury's, I wipe children's bottoms and pay taxes.

In claiming it is bourgeois to shop at Sainsbury's, participate in child care and pay taxes, Self actively contributes to the implosion of meaning because these delights have long characterised the media saturated life of the receptive masses. Likewise, Self implies that his work is authentic because he uses recreational drugs, as if those who celebrate simulation are averse to these hallucinatory stimulations. Self's reliance on productionist schemas is readily evident in his need to moralistically justify his use of heroin on the grounds that it enables him to write a particular type of novel. Equally, the fact that in the Davies interview Self talks about his work being "extreme" merely demonstrates the evanescence of speech itself, the re-absorption of the whole dialectic of communication in a total circularity of the model, of the implosion of the social in the masses. Extremism is always positional, Self's work can only be 'extreme' in relation to something else. Once everything has become immediately transparent, visible, exposed in the raw and inexorable light of information and communication, claims of extremism become the favoured fatal strategies of those still suffering from nostalgia for authenticity and signification. The opposition 'mainstream'/'extreme' being rational and not natural, structural and not factual, relational and not substantial, traces an axis of reference inside a system that Self declares he opposes while simultaneously describing what he does not wish to say, his absorption and disappearance within this system of coding.

Will Self's employment of the jargon of authenticity resonates with the rhetoric used to promote the Street Fictions conference. It should go without saying that a desire for authenticity can never be a sign of the absence of the real, since all representations have always and already been absorbed by simulation. Because 'street fiction' is predicated on images of the 'authentic,' those who are self-consciously attempting to (re)produce themselves through this trope must vigilantly avoid addressing its disappearance since their entire strategy rests upon representing simulation as 'false', and therefore incapable of enveloping the entire edifice of representation as a simulacrum.

Thus while the 'post-modern' writing that the publicity material for this conference suggested 'street fiction' was reacting against eroded the boundaries between 'novelists' and 'critics', 'readers' and 'writers' (&c.), rhetoric predicated on the 'authentic' seeks to deny the disappearance of the real without directly addressing the fact that we have witnessed a total breakdown of signification.

This 'post-modern' erosion of boundaries contributed to the disappearance of the academy, whereas 'street fiction' provides the academy with its simulated 'other.' The fact that it is now circulating images of 'the street' demonstrates that the virtual academy is vainly resorting to dissimulation – presenting the true as a moment of the false – to escape the erosion of meaning within contagious hyper-reality. By linking 'street fiction' to the city, the publicity for this conference implicitly and vainly assumed that a meaningful distinction could still be made between the rural and the urban. The city and the countryside no longer exist, they have been outstripped by a simulacrum called suburbia. Images have ceased to be viable, Englishness can no longer be animated by them. In its now triumphant suburban form, the pastoral openly flaunts the fact that it is a simulation – 'mock Tudor' being its favoured guise. Since an image is the sum total of all England ever was or could become, this crisis of representation enables us to state without fear of contradiction that England does not and never will exist. The cool universe of digitality has absorbed the world of metaphor and metonymy; the pleasure principle and the reality principle have been replaced by contagious hyperreality.

Notes for a lecture at the *Street Fictions* conference in Brighton 16 May 1998 organised by Do Tongues and Sussex University

1. For example, in *The Country And The City,* the vividness with which Williams depicts the village of his boyhood contrasts starkly with his sketchy depiction of the Cambridgeshire countryside he encountered in later life, and this perfunctory treatment of the Fens appears yet the more surprising given the professor's rhetoric against literary abstraction within the pastoral tradition. This might be taken as confirmation of the simulationist model used to structure the argument in much of my lecture.

2. Included in *Rising In The East: The Regeneration Of East London* edited by Tim Butler and Michael Rustin (Lawrence & Wishart, London 1996, p. 23).

3. Included in *Rising In The East* ibid, p. 86.

4. Sinclair is fascinated by the meaninglessness of celebrity. In the TV films he has made with Chris Petit, Sinclair has his own set of Superstars who range from secondhand book dealers to writers such as Alan Moore, Robin Cook, even myself. More recently, Sinclair has penned profiles of the super rich such as Peter Ackroyd and Lord Archer, just as Warhol made his portraits of businessmen. Sinclair's refusal to assume positions on anything is disliked by those who vainly hope to inscribe the world with meaning. After a series of press screenings for *The Falconer,* Sinclair superstar Peter Whitehead issued the following statement: "The film *The Falconer* is a work of pure fiction, in which I acted and improvised a part written for me by Sinclair. The film bears virtually no resemblance to my real life, and pays scant serious reference to my work as a film-maker, falconer or novelist. If anything, the main character seems to have been based on Milton Croockshank, the author and principle protagonist in my recent novel *Pulp Election.*" This statement is meaningless, since Whitehead himself is a work of fiction. There is no distance, not even that of objective irony, between Whitehead and Milton Croockshank.

5. The authors of the novel are Robert Dellar, Ted Curtis, Martin Cooper, Rob Colson, Lucy Williams, Mally Mallinson and Emma McElwee.

ROYAL WATCH: THE LAST CRUSADE

AFTER FOUR HUNDRED ODD YEARS in which the Vatican and the British monarchy have attempted to out-manoeuvre each other on the geo-political field, each of these combatants is fatally weakened. New powers are emerging who believe that it is their turn to control the destiny of the world. The British commonwealth is falling apart, with republican support swelling in Australia and the Caribbean. If South Africa places itself once again under the dominion of the House of Windsor, this is merely a temporary aberration, an exception that proves the rule.

Meanwhile, the Vatican is losing its grip on power in traditional strongholds such as Ireland. The case of Father Brendan Smyth is just the latest in a long series of paedophile scandals to rock the Irish Church. Naturally, the mainstream media fails to report that the ritual abuse of children forms part of an occult operation designed to restore the glory of the Catholic Church. Nevertheless, without knowing the full background to these botched ritual workings, the Irish masses are revolted by the utter corruption of their religious leaders and, as a consequence, the Church's grip on the state has been severely weakened. The decline of Irish theocracy is evident from the passing of bills that liberalise the law with regard to both homosexuality and abortion, something which the Catholic hierarchy vehemently opposes. Meanwhile, the US government, which has completely broken with its long time mentors in the Royal Family and the City of London, is looking to Eire as a potential military base from where it can do battle with its chief rival in the northern hemisphere, the newly united

Germany – hence Clinton's rapprochement with Gerry Adams.

Prince Charles is so angry with the US government for refusing orders from his family that he lambasted Americans for the way they speak English at a recent British Council reception. The barmy heir to the throne was widely reported as saying: "People tend to invent all sorts of nouns and verbs and make words that shouldn't be. I think we have to be a bit careful, otherwise the whole thing can get rather a mess." The loony pro-Catholic Académie Française saw the prince's intervention as an opportunity to wreck the English language by halting its mutational development, something they've already done for their own tongue, and were quick to get an article published in the Spring issue of *The Author*, the trade journal for British writers.

In this piece, arch Catholic reactionary Maurice Druon ranted: "What disturbs and alarms us is the parallel erosion of our two languages. Loose your language and you loose your soul... we would like to make sure that our two languages retained a touch of dignity. The vocabulary and syntax of both our languages are polluted by an idiom derived from English which I call anglo-ricain, Amerenglish. It flows like a dark tide through the audio-visual media... a jumble of abbreviations, quasi-phonetically simplified spellings, slap-dash neologisms, botched etymology, grammar disregarded, vulgarity promoted... It triumphs because it is the language of the dollar... What is to be done... in order to check the rising tide of pollution in the northern hemisphere?"

This attempt to entice Charles into the Catholic camp was doomed to failure because his head was already turned elsewhere. Charles has tired of sodomising young boys in his satanic rituals, and he's sick to the guts that these magickal workings have failed to bring about a world-wide occult theocracy headed by the House of Windsor. In desperation, the Prince has gone back to the source of Western ritual magick, those Islamic-cum-Sufi practices that were picked up by the

Templars during the twelfth-century crusades and then passed on in a corrupted form to the Freemasons. In particular, Charles has given himself over to 'imaginal yoga and sacred paedophilia'. In other words, he's now utilising the utterly sick Persian practice of contemplating young boys as sex objects, while simultaneously resisting the hormonal urges this creates and instead using the resultant sexual energy for magickal purposes. Nevertheless, at the end of the day, the innocent children rounded up for the Prince's amusement are still murdered to prevent them from exposing his sick perversions.

This is why Charlie told a London conference on Britain's place in the world that the country should learn to appreciate Islamic culture and become a "bridge builder" between Muslims and the West. 'This," the Prince went on to say, "could not be done without a willingness on our part to learn from the world of Islam and to balance our innate pragmatism with an acute awareness of the vital importance of the things of the Spirit." This is a last crusade for the monarchy, which wants to return to the source of its magickal powers and thereby renew them. The problem Prince Charles faces is that this source is itself exhausted. While Europe needed the knowledge that seeped into its feudal society from the Arab world to pull itself out of the dark ages, the Middle East long ago ceased to be the home of the most advanced civilisation known to man. The House of Windsor's days are numbered. With the Vatican finding itself in the same predicament, the future of our world lies on the Pacific Rim.

First published in *Underground 6,* Summer 1995

WE HAVE BREWED BEER: HAVE A DRINK

IN THE 1950s members of the Lettrist International used to play a psychogeographical game known as 'the possible appointment'. A subject is asked to find themselves alone, at a precise time, in a preordained place. I was one of several people tricked into playing variants on this game by Fabian Tompsett as part of his contribution to the first show at Info Centre in Hackney. Tompsett phoned me and suggested we meet at an address on Mare Street. The rendezvous turned out to be a Chinese restaurant and I was eventually thrown out after being told I couldn't wait for someone without ordering food. When I got home, I found a message from Tompsett on my answer machine telling me to go to a different address on Mare Street.

I made my way back to Hackney but instead of meeting Tompsett, I was given a meal by Henriette Heise and Jakob Jakobsen, who were in the process of setting up Info Centre with financial assistance from the Danish Contemporary Art Foundation. Henriette explained that the first Info Centre show would feature work produced by Tompsett under the aegis of the London Psychogeographical Association (LPA). Jakob told me that although Info Centre was an exhibition space, its most important function was to enable artists to meet each other and exchange ideas. This, he assured me, was the real art.

I made another telephone arrangement to meet Tompsett at Info Centre. I arrived on time but he wasn't about. It transpired he'd arranged to meet other people earlier but missed the appointments. Since the inaugural Info Centre show was on, I decided to wait around and see what happened. Gradually, more and more people arrived saying they'd arranged to meet Fabian.

Clearly, Tompsett's non-appearance had been carefully planned. His absence amplified awareness of him, and there was much speculative talk about the wily psychogeographer.

Amidst this buzz of conversation, I took in the work being shown. The main space featured boards with maps and plans attached, plus a table spread with literature. Various documents detailed the activities of the LPA, while a supplementary text explained: "In truth, it was only the East London Section which could be said to have any real kind of life. The South London Section never moved beyond having some business cards printed, the North London Section never went beyond half-hearted conversation, and there was always deep reservations about setting up a West London Section." During the five years in which the LPA issued manifestos and organised events, Tompsett was its only member. Given this, responses to the LPA ranging from articles in the national press to left-communist denunciations of the 'group' as 'political parasites' are often side-splittingly funny. However, to describe the project documented at Info Centre as merely a hoax would be extremely reductive.

Almost as perplexing as the LPA's output is the collaborative work of architect Birgitte Louise Hansen and artist Joep van Lieshout. In material documenting plans for a dysutopian city called Free State Almere, it is claimed: "Citizens settle any place in the city in mobile homes and survival wagons... The economy is concerned with the trade of weapons, alcohol and drugs. The most important part of the income for 'Free State Almere' is the prisoner camps. Against payment prisoners are brought from all over Europe to work the land." Hansen and Lieshout's work has many historical resonances, most immediately as a satirical response to several hundred years of planned – and occasionally partially realised – utopian cities. However, Free State Almere simultaneously exposes the source of the wealth – weapons, drugs and slaves – with which major European cities such as Bristol and Amsterdam were actually built.

In a separate video room, a silent tape showed Henriette Heise endlessly constructing or deconstructing a television. The film ran backwards so that it appeared a television was being put together, when it was actually being taken apart. Jakob Jakobsen's work also touched on the construction of the social. The beer he was brewing would carry on fermenting until the end of the show, when those who'd visited the exhibition were invited to come back and drink it. The beer is a good illustration of Info Centre's ongoing commitment to social process and disdainful attitude towards commodified culture. It will be interesting to see what they do next.

Previously published in *AN Magazine*, July 1998

HOW TO BE AN ART TART

CAN YOU NAME all the recent winners of the Booker Prize, BP Portrait Award, Whitbread Prize, *Evening Standard* Drama Awards and Mercury Music Prize? If the answer is yes, you're obviously a pundit. Most people remember the names of awards rather than the winners. This is why arts prizes are proliferating at an alarming rate – they are a very attractive proposition to business sponsors. Gone are days when writers, musicians and painters could sign on the dole to gain the time they needed to develop their ideas. Instead, welfare cuts are forcing increasing numbers of people to chase after ever diminishing arts grants. Art funding is now like playing the lottery; but it's a game which is loaded in favour of clued-up players. In 1993, Rachel Whiteread won the Turner Prize for being the best artist of the year and more tellingly, the K Foundation award for being the worst. If Rachel Whiteread, the worst artist of 1993, can scoop the Turner Prize, then you can win the arts award of your choice. Here's how to do it.

1. MEDIOCRITY: Anything arousing strong feelings is likely to be rejected by a prize committee. Original and imaginative works never win awards. Rather than favouring creative excellence, consensus decision-making foregrounds whatever is found least objectionable by the entire committee. When Seamus Heaney won the Noble Prize for Literature, his poetry was praised for it's "lyrical beauty," what this really meant was that it was unlikely to offend anyone.

2. NEPOTISM: Nothing beats the 'old boy' network as a short cut to success, as the art world success of Damien Hirst and his

Goldsmiths College peers demonstrates. Asked to choose between an acquaintance and somebody they don't know, most people will award prizes to their friends. The upshot of this is that you have to go out and press the flesh at launches and prize givings. Even when you're not up for an award, it is essential that you attend industry events.

3. FLATTERY: Will Self cultivated the literary establishment and managed to get himself selected as one of Granta's 20 Best Young British Novelists before his first full-length book had been published! Swallow your pride and ape the behaviour of a teacher's pet. It is essential that you massage the egos of the committee members awarding the prize you covet. Prize juries won't pick winners who rock the boat.

4. MANNERS: Regardless of your social origins, you must reinvent yourself as middle-class. A typical pre-Turner Prize meal consists of mille feuille of griddled aubergine with goats cheese and bressaola, boned roast quail with wild mushrooms plus an eighteen item pudding buffet. Your friends in the world of culture don't want to be embarrassed by some yob who demands brown sauce and doesn't know how to hold a knife and fork!

5. RELIABILITY: Prize juries want winners they can depend upon. Since all branches of the culture industry are riddled with factional rivalries, you must make your loyalties clear. If you favour *The London Review Of Books,* then you must be against *The Times Literary Supplement*. Obviously, your loyalties influence which prizes you stand a chance of winning.

6. DUPLICITY: Prize juries like to think their taste is more sophisticated than that of the average punter. Artists and writers who upset knee-jerk conservatives provide award-givers with an opportunity to display their 'progressive' taste. Take a leaf out of Umberto Eco's book – the trick is to upset critics like Brian Sewell and Auberon Waugh, without doing anything a liberal would find difficult to stomach.

7. DISPOSABILITY: We live in the age of the sound-bite, so forget about great themes like time, death and eternity. Visitors to the Tate stand in front of a painting for an average of three seconds, this is down from seven seconds ten years ago. Similarly reviewers and prize juries don't have time to give contemporary culture proper consideration, so produce something that will grab their attention. Gilbert & George are a perfect example of this.

8. FAMILIARITY: Imitation is the sincerest form of flattery and everybody likes what they already know. Oasis scooped the 1996 Brit Awards thanks to their skill at rehashing old Beatles riffs, while Douglas Gordon has been honoured for his fifth-rate conceptualism. Don't waste your time searching for a style of your own, copy somebody else.

9. MODESTY: Everybody loves a 'good' winner. You must express surprise at your success, so that the public remains ignorant of the extensive lobbying that went on prior to the jury awarding you the prize. Praise the work of those who lost. By adopting a pose of humility, you consolidate the power and influence bestowed upon you by a major award.

10. REALISM: Rather than belonging to the cultural realm, awards and prizes are an adjunct to Thatcherism. Don't be mislead into believing they have anything to do with artistic merit. Experimental and creative works are being marginalised as culture becomes increasingly dominated by the institutions that dole out art prizes. The best model for success within this field is business competition. Rather than using strenuous defensive measures to conceal the flimsiness of your achievements, be bold, brazen and shameless. Keep your mind fixed on the honours that accompany success – only bohemian losers worry about the content of their cultural productions.

First published in *The Big Issue*, 17-23 February 1997

DENNIS COOPER DOES DRUGS

THE POLO BAR on Bishopsgate is open twenty-four hours a day. The coffee is variable, so I usually order tea. I arranged to meet Dennis Cooper in this particular café because it is conveniently close to Liverpool Street station and three Jack The Ripper murder sites. Dennis is a Los Angeles based novelist whose cult fiction explores his obsessional interest in young boys, sex murder, turds and bad pop music. Cooper's latest novel *Guide* (Serpent's Tail) contains a sexually explicit sequence featuring a thinly fictionalised version of Blur bassist Alex James. Cooper agreed to meet me if I'd plug the writing of his current boyfriend Michael Tolson, a twenty year-old junkie from Pittsburgh. Michael is looking for someone to publish his novel *Crap Hound* – more about that later.

As he stumbled into the café wearing an old jacket over a white T-shirt, a pair of cords and Timberlands, Dennis looked like he fronted an indie band, specifically The Fall. However, from the way he stared in fascination at a coffee stain on our table it quickly became apparent that Cooper didn't share Fall singer Mark E. Smith's penchant for booze. For a moment I'd thought Cooper was drunk but his boyfriend quickly corrected this erroneous impression. "Dennis is tripping," Michael explained. Several minutes after I'd asked if I should order coffee, Cooper mumbled "Cool." I took this to mean yes. Michael managed to pour coffee down his throat – Dennis spilled the beverage down the front of his white T-shirt. At this point I decided to cancel an order for egg and chips. The café's staff appeared relieved as I coughed up the readies for the stuff we'd consumed and split.

It's weird to think that someone as spaced out as Dennis could get it together to write a novel. I asked him about this as we ambled down Artillery Row towards the site of Jack The Ripper's Dorset Street murder, now a multi-storey car park. My attempt to conduct an interview on the hoof was anything but satisfactory since whenever I put a question to Cooper I was lucky if I got a mono-syllabic response. When we arrived at the murder site I described the carve-up of Marie Kelly in graphic detail. Dennis didn't seem interested – his attention was absorbed by a grease-stained Kentucky Fried Chicken box he'd plucked from the gutter. "Awesome" Dennis enthused as he turned this piece of litter over in his hands. Hoping for a better reaction elsewhere, I led Dennis and Michael up to Hanbury Street where Annie Chapman had been found lying on her back, hacked to pieces.

Dennis remained unmoved by the Jack The Ripper murders. He'd removed several bones from the discarded Kentucky Fried Chicken box and was subjecting them to a rigorous examination. This culminated in Cooper crunching the bones between his teeth. When I suggested we visit the site of another Ripper atrocity, Michael explained that Dennis was only interested in the murder of young boys and found hetero sex crime boring. Cooper was completely fried and there was no way he'd give me a coherent interview, so I put him in a taxi and told the driver to take him to Joshua Compston's flat on the Kingsmead Estate in Homerton. Compston was a Brit Art wannabe and two time loser, so I assumed he'd know the exact location of the notorious rent boy murder that took place very close to his pad a few years back. Young boys aren't my thing, but I was left standing at the corner of Hanbury and Commercial Street with Michael as Cooper's taxi zoomed off.

"You can fuck me for the price of a fix," Michael announced once Dennis had disappeared into the London traffic.

"I'm straight," I explained.

"You're on another planet," Michael shot back.

The kid might have been a permanent emotional wreck, but he was sharp in the semi-educated manner of a teenage runaway who'd dropped out of school after reading a dozen William Burroughs books. Eventually we came to an agreement – I'd pay Michael £15 to have sex with a girl. Finding the girl wasn't difficult. She was nineteen and hooked on crack. Sabrina was wearing white shoes, dirty Levis, a matted sweater and her tangled black hair was a mess. Her beat was Commercial Street and her price was £20. We took a cab to a derelict property on Old Street. I'd acquired a set of keys to the building from a friend in need of a score. In the taxi Michael pulled a copy of his novel from a bag and handed it to me. This was useful since it gave me something to read as he shagged Sabrina. I didn't want to watch them get it on. Keeping Michael sweet was simply a way of staying tight with Dennis.

When Sabrina undressed I could see that her sallow skin matched Michael's junkie pallor. I focused my attention on the opening of Tolson's manuscript: "I'd concealed myself in a doorway to do some investigative research by observing the punters going into Huysmans, a porno store in Hollywood. To help pass the time I fondled my parts. Eventually I clocked cult novelist Dennis Cooper scuttling inside. He was carrying a large box filled with old paedophile magazines. I instantly came in my pants. Twenty minutes passed before Cooper was out on the street again. I'd already come so the only way I could express my tremendous excitement was by shitting myself. A crack hooker standing nearby pulled a face and stomped off down the street complaining about scum lowering the tone of the neighbourhood. Striding across the road towards the object of my lust, I savoured the delicious sensation of excrement oozing down my legs."

The novel turned out to be a parochial beat effort. Imagine William Burroughs plagiarised by a porno hack who spends their spare time reading Harold Robbins and fantasising about making it with rock stars. I threw the manuscript down, placed seven five pound notes on top of it and slipped out of the building while Michael was still grinding away on top of Sabrina. I've heard that somehow Dennis Cooper made it back to LA and is writing for the American rock press. I've no idea what happened to his boyfriend.

First published in *Headpress 17*, Summer 1998

THE SATANGATE TAPES

AT ABOUT 8PM on January 27th 1993 I noticed the call light was flashing on my telephone answering machine. Playing back the message, I immediately recognised the voices of Prince Charles and Sir Laurens van der Post. They were obviously conducting a private conversation and I was left wondering how the hell their phone call had found its way onto my answering machine. Had there been a crossed line or was I being set up by MI5 and the Press Complaints Commission? Since it's pointless speculating on how the conversation ended up on my answering machine, I'll simply provide a transcript of what was said.

Charles: Battersea Dogs Home.
Laurens: Charlie, it's Laurens van der Post, for God's sake grow up, I'm sick of your schoolboy jokes.
Charles: Hail Satan!
Laurens: Hail Satan!
Charles: Hail Satan!
Laurens: Pull yourself together, I've rung up to talk about the ritual we'll do at the equinox to put you in touch with your secret chief.
Charles: Hail Satan!
Laurens: You'll have to deflower ten virgins during the hours of darkness. Do you think you're up to it?
Charles: Hail Satan!
Laurens: For God's sake answer the question!
Charles: Everything will be dandy, I'll steal papa's delay spray, that'll see me through the ritual.

Laurens: It's difficult procuring virgins these days, so I'm going to kidnap some schoolgirls.

Charles: Oh Laurens, you know I prefer older women, can't you find me some nice matrons?

Laurens: How could we be sure they were virgins? People are so dishonest these days.

Charles: You know I hate children. You know I murdered hundreds of them in a previous life as Gilles de Rais.

Laurens: I've told you before Charlie, I've done a lot of research into the psychic bloodline of your family and you weren't Gilles de Rais in a previous life. It was your brother Andrew who was Gilles de Rais.

Charles: Andrew was never Gilles de Rais, it was me! Me!

Laurens: Let's just forget about it and run through a few details we need to sort out before the equinox ritual.

Charles: Hail Satan!

Laurens: Have you been charging your magical wand with ancient earth energies?

Charles: Hail Satan!

Laurens: Charlie, I read in the paper that a woman got brain cancer from the signals given off by her mobile phone. Do you think you've been over using yours? Have you had dizzy spells or anything like that?

Charles: Hail Satan!

Laurens: Have you been overworking? Do you feel under a lot of pressure?

Charles: Hail Satan!

Laurens: We're really not getting anywhere with this conversation.

Charles: Hail Satan!

Laurens: I'm very worried about you Charlie.

Charles: Hail Satan!

Laurens: In fact I'm going to come and see you. It'll take a few hours but I'm coming over to help you sort yourself out. Don't touch that mobile phone before I arrive.

Charles: Hail Satan!

Laurens: I'll be over soon.

Charles: Hail Satan!

Laurens: You really need to get back in touch with nature. You need to focus your thoughts. Some alchemical speculation might do you good until I can get you out into the wilds of Africa.

Charles: Hail Satan!

Laurens: Do you remember what I told you about Jung?

Charles: Hail Satan!

Laurens: Charlie, you need to get off that mobile phone immediately. I'll be right over.

Charles: Hail Satan!

Laurens: I'll be over in about four hours.

Charles: Hail Satan!

Laurens: Bye.

Charles: Hail Satan!

Laurens: Bye.

Charles: Hail Satan!

That's it, the whole tape. The sheer banality of the conversation seems to prove its authenticity. An exchange that's so absurd has to be genuine. Possibly there's a conspiracy afoot to get the contents of this telephone call published. But even if this is the case, the people of Britain should know that as a disciple of Satan, Prince Charles is not fit to be their king.

Previously published in the pamphlet
Conspiracies, Cover-Ups & Diversions by Stewart Home
(Sabotage Editions, 1995)

THE ECLIPSE AND RE-EMERGENCE OF THE COMMODITY FORM

THE ONGOING EROSION of the modernist defence of the 'critical autonomy of art' has been reflected in changing attitudes towards popular culture. While some critics have campaigned for the incorporation of 'classic' examples of popular culture into the canon of art, others have extended their critiques of commodity aesthetics into the realm of serious culture. However, most have adopted positions that fall either between or outside the two poles I've just established. For example, an extremely low-grade restatement of Adorno is currently being combined with a celebration of the 'transgressive' by the circle of fledgling failures centred on the Frankfurt School groupie John 'Porno' Roberts. I have dealt with Roberts elsewhere, so here I will briefly examine some writing by his acolyte Robert Garnett.

In 'Beyond The Hype' (*Art Monthly 196,* April 1996), Garnett claimed that "in the 80s, the 'low' was something one appropriated rather than experienced and enjoyed. This can partly explain the impetus behind the carnivalesque indulgence with the base and the 'low' and the autobiographical impulse that motivates such artists as Georgina Starr and Tracey Emin, and the sense of liberation from the strictures of political rectitude that Sarah Lucas's work articulates." Despite the use of ironising quote marks, Garnett's statement clearly absolutises the 'low' rather than treating it as something which is positional. Considered positionally, the 'low' and 'base' are always something one experiences as other and are thus appropriated, rather than directly experienced.

To someone who listens exclusively to classical music, The Who are 'low'. A Who fan may well consider Slade 'low'. A Slade fan might view Oasis as 'low'. An Oasis fan probably thinks East 17 are 'low'. For an East 17 fan, their grandparent's Roy Orbison and Jim Reeves records are likely to be seen as 'low'. Similarly, an alcoholic can consider junkies 'low', while those shooting smack can look down on crackheads. There are manifestations of popular culture, such as jokes, that deal with these forms of 'distinction' both explicitly and elliptically: "A doctor tells a patient that he has two pieces of bad news. You have both cancer and Alzheimer's Disease. The patient replies that's terrible, I have cancer. Oh well, at least I don't have Alzheimer's."

Returning to Garnett, having brought up Tracy Emin, the 'low' and the autobiographical, this hapless 'theorist' concludes his piece by talking about the reflexivity of art, distinguishing it from forms of popular culture such as punk rock. One of Emin's best known works is *Everyone I Ever Slept With,* which prominently features the name of the rock musician Billy Childish. If, to Garnett, punk rock represents the 'low' in contrast to the reflexivity of art, then how is he to position the autobiographical when Tracey Emin's public visibility in the eighties was largely based on her being the girlfriend of garage musician Billy Childish? What's more, Emin has made use of this association in her nineties art works.

Indeed, not only did Childish publish some of Emin's early writing and drawing in *Six Turkish Tales* (Hangman Books, Rochester 1987), under the name Dolli Bambi her mistreatment at his hands is detailed in numerous songs and poems. The single *Dolli Bambi* enumerates some of the 'bad' things Childish did to Emin; much of it is surprisingly mild, such as fucking her up the arse. Rather than being something new and unique to nineties Britain as both Garnett and John Roberts absurdly claim, the autobiographical/confessional discourse within which Emin operates can be traced back through Childish's poems, fiction and lyrics, to this rock musician's literary influences such as

Charles Bukowski and Louis-Ferdinand Céline.

Childish, as his name implies, prides himself on his amateurism. Despite this, he is one of the few professionals – as well as being the biggest star – on the garage rock scene today. Childish's output is both idiosyncratic and bizarrely industrial. Having produced more than 70 full length albums in twenty years, Childish has a thing about shitting out product. His group, Thee Headcoats, don't rehearse, treating their monthly gigs in London as ample preparation for their frequent foreign tours. Headcoats albums usually consist of either twelve or fourteen songs with a playing time of around half an hour. The records are always recorded at the Toe-Rag Studios in London on analogue eight-track gear. Headcoats recordings are cheap to make, the songs are all based on a few simple structures which are shoe-horned into one basic sound. I'm not trying to put Childish down; his output might be a beat and a few chords but I love it. His amped up guitar sound is derived from the work of Link Wray and Bo Diddley, while the group's humorous image is heavily influenced by the British beat combo The Downliners Sect.

Don Craine of the Downliners Sect always wore a deerstalker hat, referred to as his 'headcoat', in songs such as *Leader Of The Sect,* a parody of The Shangri-Las' *Leader Of The Pack*. Artists desiring fame require an easily recognisable trade-mark by which the public can recognise them. This might be anything from Bill Hailey's kiss curl to the eye-patch worn by both Johnny Kid and Gabrielle. The Downliners Sect adopted the deerstalker as their gimmick. Aside from naming his current band after Don's 'headcoat', and dressing up in similar gear, Childish has parodied Downliners Sect record titles. Indeed, Thee Headcoats have even made an album with the current incarnation of The Downliners Sect. Likewise, Tracy Emin isn't the only person to gain her initial public exposure through Childish's industrious family-style business. As well as fronting Thee Headcoats, Childish and his band act as backing musicians to Thee Headcoatees, a girl vocal group featuring Thee

Headcoats' current and former girlfriends.

Childish's up-front attitude about where he finds inspiration means that those who adhere to the 'rock music as art' thesis tend to ignore him. Despite the hype surrounding the advent of so called 'post-modernism', 'originality' is still fetishised by adherents to both popular and serious culture. Commodification leads to genre differentiation being used to segment the market and create niche selling-pitches, which in its turn necessitates that different forms of music are based on easily recognisable sound structures. Rock music is made from largely interchangeable sections called riffs, which joined together make a complete song. There are a handful of basic chord progressions used within all rock tunes. Within popular music, genre differentiation comes down to fairly minor variations of sound. A key difference between late-seventies punk rock and eighties hardcore was that the latter speeded up the beat and put the drums up in the mix while taking the vocals down, making the overall sound more rhythmic and less melodic. Nevertheless, the music was still guitar based and used the same chord patterns.

The Ramones, who stripped down the rock sound and thus became one of the seminal late-seventies punk groups, provide a fine example of how chord patterns are used to create songs. The Ramones always used 4/4 time, and within this structure they placed simple, recurring chord progressions. The chord patterns in Ramones songs correspond to those that already existed in pop music before the band was formed. The progressions are simply lifted and adapted from tunes of the 1950s and 1960s. The chord sequence in *Blitzkreig Bop* is a copy of *Twist And Shout,* the verse of *Chainsaw* is a partial rip-off of *His Latest Flame.* This is indicative of the fact that the construction of popular music is a process based on producing new work from the unitary elements of past songs.

In view of this, the controversy surrounding the partial re-assignment of copyright to The Stranglers of a song by Elastica, appears particularly ridiculous. In contemporary sampled dance music the process of appropriation is even more blatant. Composition still begins with the selection of the musical units to be revalorised, but the tedious necessity of mastering an instrument on which to recreate riffs is avoided. Constructing new works from past elements is in no way unique to either music or popular culture. A similar analysis could be made of this lecture, where one might make reference to Pierre Bourdieu's book *Distinction: A Social Critique Of The Judgement Of Taste* and the musicology in Dave Laing's *One Chord Wonders: Power And Meaning In Punk Rock*.

Although both popular and serious culture are products of commodification surprisingly little has been written about the entanglement of pop music and the automobile industry. Records have traditionally been made from vinyl which is a by-product of petroleum. The expansion of the modern music industry was fuelled by the need to find ways of turning extra profit from the exploitation of oil reserves. There is still much to be written on the importance of the car as a favoured choice of subject matter within rock songs. Both cars and youth culture are sold on the premise that they offer those who consume them freedom. This marketing strategy has not been affected by the switch from vinyl to CD formats. The CD represents a quantum leap as far as the commodity form of music is concerned, since it is more compact than vinyl records and one does not have to get up to turn a CD over after a mere twenty or so minutes.

Nevertheless, it is necessary to avoid falling into the trap of over-emphasising the exchange-value of commercial products and thus ignoring the fact that to function commodities must also have a use value, even if this is principally symbolic. Obviously, music has a physiological effect on the listener. Just as importantly, rock culture provides a stimulus for the subjectivity of those who 'consume' it. This provides one of the main focuses of interest in publications such as the *NME* and *Melody Maker,* where genre mutations are fastidiously recorded. While there is a blurring of boundaries between consumers and producers within the field of popular music, well illustrated by the way in which rock songs are conjured up out of past works, what we have here looks remarkably similar to what Roland Barthes announced as the death of the author and the birth of the reader.

From this perspective, the 'radical' rhetoric of anarchist rock groups like Crass is exposed as no more than a pose. Crass sold themselves on their 'authenticity,' and conned their audience into believing they were getting 'value for money' because the group undercut the major record companies. Crass vilified 'big business' while assiduously propagating the commodity form upon which capitalism is predicated! Since Crass sold themselves on the basis of single 'obvious' and 'predominant' 'meanings' within their work, they simultaneously inhibited the use of their records as a stimulus for the free play of human subjectivity. In as far as Crass indulged this 'demonstrative impulse' and succeeded in imposing it upon their fans, they undermined the use value – and thus also the exchange value – of their records. Thus despite undercutting 'big capital', Crass did not provide 'value for money.' As is still the case with budget repackagers of commercial music, flogging records 'cheap' was simply the means by which Crass shifted shoddy product.

While projecting itself as an alternative to dominant ideologies, anarchism – in the UK at least – is a form of white identity politics rooted in the ideology of the aesthetic. Obviously, the political situation in, for example, the Middle East results in the anarchist ideology taking on a different cast when it is advocated by individuals whose social positions enable them to experiment with beliefs of this type. I can certainly sympathise with the motivations that I understand to have led the Israeli anarcho-punk band Nekhei Naatza to release the EP *Renounce Judaism* in 1994. However, the fact that the record was issued by the American Beer City label makes me deeply uneasy, since the consumption of such releases within an over-integrated youth subculture around the world has been rendered particularly problematic by the not insignificant role English anarcho-punk groups have played in deforming and retarding the development of radical social movements.

On the subject of assimilation, Steve Cohen observes in *That's Funny, You Don't Look Anti-Semitic: An Anti-Racist Analysis Of Left Anti-Semitism* that the "advice that Jews should assimilate in order to avoid 'programs' is startlingly reactionary for various reasons... the Left echoes the Jewish establishment, which also advocates assimilation as a way of avoiding political struggles against anti-semitism. Indeed, the Left is articulating a position which is almost identical to the 'aspects' of zionism that it attacks with the most vehemence. Thus zionism is seen as an avoidance of the necessity to fight against anti-semitism – but this is precisely what assimilation is. Furthermore zionism is criticised for presupposing an 'eternal anti-semite' who cannot be confronted but must be by-passed through the creation of some form of national ghetto. In a sense, Lenin's position is even more extreme. He seems to believe in the eternal anti-semite whom Jews can neither confront nor avoid but can only satisfy by *un*becoming Jewish."

I do not consider it necessary to take seriously those critics who claim that Oasis are more radical than The Spice Girls, or that Tricky is more subversive than Jim Reeves. It is not Tricky or Jim Reeves who are subversive but the imaginations of the individuals who subjectively respond to their works. Indeed, contra Garnett, it becomes pointless to distinguish between popular and serious culture in terms of 'reflexivity'; a more satisfactory explanation of their differences can be found in the institutional apparatus that surrounds them. Genres such as opera and jazz were at one time considered popular but now belong to the realm of serious culture. Institutional explanations of culture provide a model that can deal with the elevation of popular forms to the status of art. The same cannot be said for Garnett's strangely static notion of 'reflexivity' or the reactionary platitudes propagated by Crass.

Notes for a lecture at Ruskin College, Oxford, 4 March 1997

BIKE BOYS, SKINHEADS AND DRUNKEN HACKS

Laurence James interviewed by Stewart Home at the Creation Books office, Clerkenwell, 9 August 1994.

AMONG OTHER THINGS, Laurence James is the author of the legendary 'Mick Norman' Hell's Angels books, which rank among the best English language youthsploitation novels of all time. Before becoming a full time writer, James worked at New English Library where he edited the early Richard Allen books and a lot else to boot. The four Mick Norman novels – *Angels From Hell, Angel Challenge, Guardian Angels* and *Angels On My Mind* – were very successfully republished in an omnibus edition by Creation Books in 1994. I talked to Laurence James shortly after the Mick Norman books were reissued, but the disappearance of the tapes prevented me from doing anything with the interview. By the time Simon Strong returned the two 90 minute cassettes to me six months later, I'd missed my deadline for *The Modern Review* and was in no rush to transcribe them. Instead, I consoled myself with the thought that at least Simon had satiated his curiosity about the author of his favourite Hell's Angels novels. Recently, I stumbled across an analysis of the 'Mick Norman' output in *British Low Culture: From Safari Suits To Sexploitation* by Leon Hunt (Routledge, London & New York 1998, p. 74-90) and decided it was time to dust down the Laurence James interview tapes.

Shortly after this interview Laurence's health collapsed. He was taken into hospital in Oxford, where he now lives, with chronic renal failure. This was diagnosed as being linked to terminal myeloma, or bone cancer, and he was given a prognosis of no more than a couple of years to live. During this period he finished off existing contracts but took on no new work. In the autumn of 1997, well past his literal deadline, his specialists told him that he didn't have terminal cancer, and indeed had never had it. It had been confused with an extremely rare condition called light chain deposition. So, currently, he is hoping to be put on the waiting list for a possible kidney transplant. He is now looking forward to resuming writing, concentrating this time on children's books.

Home: Where did you grow up?

James: In the Midlands. I was born in West Bromwich and I spent my first 18 years in Birmingham which is why quite a chunk of the Angels quartet is set in and around Birmingham. I went to a minor public school there.

Home: Which one?

James: King Edward's.

Home: It's notorious because Tory racist Enoch Powell is an ex-pupil.

James: It's a place that always finishes at number two or number three in the league tables for state scholarships to Oxford and Cambridge. It's a great scholarship school. I wasn't very successful. Rather than going on to Oxford or Cambridge, I finished up training as a PE teacher at Goldsmith's in New Cross because I didn't have the Latin, which was a shame. After a year, I decided teaching was not for me and I went to work in Foyles bookshop.

Home: So when was it that you came to London?

James: I came down to London at the beginning of the sixties and dropped out of college about '62, Then I worked in Foyles and Harrods, that was in my short hair days. After that I worked in publishing for ten years off and on till about 1970 when I went to New English Library and ran the editorial side of NEL for three years.

Home: So where were you working before NEL?

James: Before NEL I was working for a firm called Leslie Frewin.

Home: What sort of operation was it?

James: It started off as a small publisher and was very successful, but then, as time went by, every year there'd be slightly more put out: six books, then twelve books, then 24 books. There's a point at which you're not getting good product in at all and Leslie Frewin reached that point and he carried on publishing. I was really sorry he went bust.

Home: You were in London in the sixties, rumour has it there was a lot happening.

James: There wasn't a lot happening in Hither Green. Not down in south London. I hung around with a lot of friends living down in New Cross. I had a girlfriend down there at the time. I don't think very much was happening outside the centre. It wasn't a drug crazed heaven at all.

Home: But presumably every now and then you were going down some of the clubs in the west end.

James: Not very much. We tended to stay local. We tended not to go to the west end a lot. I had friends in Chelsea, so I used to go and play around there. I was playing rugby at the time as well. I was kind of rough trade for these friends in Chelsea. They had a flat just off the King's Road and they were all very nobby and I was kind of rough trade, you know what I mean. We used to play a game called Indians where you gave everybody one card face down, you pick it up and you hold it against your head and you can see everybody's card, but you can't see your own. We used to make money out of these people. We used to cheat by working together. They were terribly upper class.

Home: Did you know any of the beat-related writers like Alexander Trocchi?

James: No, I met him in a bookshop just off Charing Cross Road, Indica. Miles used to work there.

Home: Did you feel part of that scene?

James: No, it was a small literary scene. People like Ginsberg would come over, Burroughs would come over, you know and read, but it was a very tiny clique. Wholly Communion at the Albert Hall was an amazing one off. It was a good thing to go to because suddenly you realised that actually there were two and a half thousand other people in London who liked the same things as you.

Home: So this is the kind of stuff you were reading, American beats.

James: Yeah, I was working for Foyle's and my predecessor was the post manager there. I was at Foyle's for three months, I'd been there for three weeks as a post clerk. The post·manager was sacked and so the shop manager came and said, "has anybody got a degree?" and nobody had. He said "has anybody got A levels?" and I said "yes, I've got A levels". He said "right, you're post manager" and so I took over that department. And in the desk I found a copy of *Kaddish*. That was the first thing I read by Ginsberg. That was about '62 and that's when I really started reading. At NEL I got to edit a book called *Electric Underground*, which was a best of City Lights anthology, all the beats were in it. That was a great book to do.

Home: Right, so another question about the sixties is did you have any run-ins with motor cycle gangs?

James: Absolutely none, not at all. I mean what really started the motor cycle thing was Hunter S. Thompson's *Hell's Angels* book. It was very successful, and then at New English Library we published Jim Moffatt's skinhead books which were very successful, so we looked for another area of youth culture and the motor cycle gangs were an obvious area for that, and I think Peter Cave did the first ones and also a guy called Stuart Gordon who wrote some bike books under the name Alex R. Stuart. At the time I was getting disillusioned with publishing, I was not quite 30 and there wasn't really anywhere higher to go. In a sense I was almost at the top of my profession and I thought, Christ, another 35 years. This is tedious. And I'd take guys out to lunch and I'd give them ideas for books and they'd go and write them and they'd make £150, £200 out of these books, and I thought, "I could do that" and so I wrote the first Angels book and sent it in through a friend anonymously to the other editor, so I actually never touched it. NEL bought it and after that I did three more. They all did well, they sold about 70,000 copies each, which was good sales even then.

Home: Could you tell me about James Moffatt who wrote the Richard Allen skinhead books?

James: Yes, I inherited him as an author because the guy who ran NEL was Peter Haining and Moffatt had written for him, and in fact the first book I was ever involved in at NEL was a book called *Satan's Slaves*.

Home: Moffatt's highly collectable Manson cash-in.

James: That's right, the Manson book. I'd either just started at NEL, or I was about to start, and Peter Haining and his wife were round having supper at our house and we were talking about Manson and Peter said: "We'll get Jim Moffatt to do a book on the murders." And so Peter got me to ring Jim, who was living in Cheltenham at the time and I said "do you fancy doing a book about Manson?" That was all I had to say and then four days later the manuscript arrived on my desk.

Home: It's an extraordinary production because the first two chapters are about Manson and then he goes on about Aimee Semple McPherson and other people like that for most of the book.

James: That was my fault. I think he was inadequately briefed for that one. You know his research methods. The research he did for the skinhead books was like two hours in one pub talking to half a dozen skinheads. He hated skinheads, he hated kids. He was not a youth oriented man, Jim really wasn't. I can't remember now who had the idea for the skinhead series, it may have been Peter Haining. It may have been mine, it may have been Jim himself, but the first skinhead book came out and sold extremely well.

Home: The story Moffatt always told about it was that some

Chelsea fan had been commissioned to do the first book and hadn't come up with the goods, and so he got in at the last minute. I've no idea if this is true but this is his story about how he got to do the book.

James: I have no recollection of that at all. I'm not saying that's not true. But I can't remember how it did actually come up, where it came from. I can't remember the catalyst for the skinhead books but Jim started doing them, and he was a terrible old man. He was unreliable, extremely right-wing, a terrible drunk, a liar, he hated kids. What more can I tell you about Jim Moffatt?

Home: He was a talented hack with reactionary political views and a drink problem.

James: In his early days he was an extremely talented hack, a really good hack writer, but unfortunately, as it went on, he began to believe that he was in touch with youth culture. And youth culture to him was fascist skinheads. He started putting masses of terrible racism in his books. His manuscripts were just completely racist. And I was labouring away trying to get rid of all this from his prose and saying "Jim, sorry, you can't keep kicking the heads of Asians, no, sorry Jim." And in the end, after *Skinhead Girls* I actually refused to deal with him any more because of his drink problem. He'd ring me up and say "Have you got the manuscript?" and I'd say "no" and he'd say, "Well I posted it yesterday. I'll post you another copy." And I actually knew that all the time he was sleeping on the floor of his agent's office in Bloomsbury in Great Russell Street writing the books. He hadn't even started some of these books. He became terribly unreliable and in the end I wouldn't have anything to do with him. I had him moved to another editor. I'd had enough of Jim. One of the worst things for an editor is to have an author who lies to you. I mean if an author says "Look, I'm really in the shit here. Can we meet? I'm going to be three weeks late," or "I'm going to be six weeks late" or whatever. As long as he gives you warning, it's okay. But when you get an author who says, "Yeah, nearly finished it, it'll go in the post tomorrow" and this isn't true and you're bound by a production schedule for the book and you've got your slot at the printers and if you miss that slot there isn't another slot. The next slot's probably down along here. And that was a terrible problem.

Home: Do you know anything about Moffatt's father who was supposedly a serious literary writer?

James: No, he never talked about his father. I met his wife because his wife did a bit of writing as well. Jim did a lot of books apart from the skinhead series. He did *The Gold Cup Murder* set at the Cheltenham races. There was *The Sleeping Bomb* which is one of the great covers of all time. That's one of Dick Clifton Dey's first covers for NEL. The cover was wonderful. Jim did *The Marathon Murder* which was the book he supposedly wrote in a week.

Home: I've heard some interesting stories about that book because it is the one where he went on BBC2 *Late Night Line-Up* and was given a plot outline, then had to go back a week later with the completed manuscript.

James: I think it was Jim's idea to pretend to do a book under great pressure, as a media stunt.

Home: I think as far as the TV audience were concerned, Jim went on the show one week and was given a plot outline and then wrote the book in a week and then NEL got it out the week after that. I've been told that the book was written and ready for the printer before Jim was given the outline on air.

James: Yes. I mean he cheated slightly because the brief he had was very loose and sloppy and so Jim just fitted in something he was going to write anyway.

Home: How did the book actually do?

James: It was a total disaster, an utter disaster. I think we probably printed something like 100,000 and sold about 20. It seemed a good idea. Jim fulfilled his part perfectly well. He wrote a perfectly acceptable book but it had a very dull cover.

It's a perfectly competent piece of writing but Jim did get worse and worse as he went on.

Home: There are a few other figures I'd like to ask you about. Did you have anything to do with the Sam Fuller book *144 Piccadilly?*

James: That was mine. I bought that book. It didn't do very well. I thought it was a smashing book. I bought it really because I thought I'd get a chance to meet Sam Fuller and I never did. It was a lovely book.

Home: So how did you get offered it?

James: It was published in the States and it was sent by an agent in a big box of stuff. I fought very hard to do it because I thought it was a great idea and there was talk of a movie as well. Sam Fuller was going to make a movie from it, which he never did and he was going to come to London which he didn't. It's a good book, an interesting book. It's clearly an American's book looking at the London situation, so in some sense, it's slightly flawed. If I wrote about Los Angeles gangs I would obviously make some mistakes and Fuller does this occasionally, he's not always quite on the ball.

Home: How many books were NEL publishing a year?

James: Probably something like 60 or 70 hardbacks and 150 to 200 paperbacks. And there were only two of us. I was working much of the time with a bloke called Mark Howell who's now editing a newspaper in Key West. We had a good time at NEL, we were doing all the commissioning, we were doing all the contracting, we were writing all the blurbs, doing any editing, proof-reading that went on as well. It was good. An astronomical amount of work.

Home: For what was supposed to have been a hack operation, you had a few writers who are now quite well respected by the literary establishment. You had Chris Priest.

James: That's right. Chris was doing hack writing all the time under a variety of names and I bought him as a serious writer, books like *Fugue For A Darkening Island*.

Home: Who wrote the NEL horror books?

James: I think they were mostly bought in from America. An agent called Singer used to handle a lot of stuff like that. Horror generally wasn't selling all that well. Not as well as science fiction in those days. We did things like re-publishing the Asimov juveniles, which weren't actually great literature but they were quite fun. They'd never been done before in England and you could sell 40,000 of them effortlessly. We did Heinlein juveniles as well.

Home: Also, you had Peter Haining at NEL who edited some very impressive horror anthologies.

James: Yes, he's a great anthologist, a brilliant anthologist. He included the first story I ever had published in one of his anthologies, a story called 'Mercy,' and it's in *The Unspeakable People* that he did for Leslie Frewin.

Home: So that was in the sixties.

James: That would have been in the late sixties. That was the first story I had published. Then I had stories published in *New Worlds* and in *Corgi New Writing* series, I had short stories published. Then I more or less gave up short story writing.

Home: Another person I wanted to ask you about was Tony Lopez who wrote a gangster series called *The Hoods* and is now a well respected academic poet.

James: He was after my time. There was a very hectic period during the early seventies when the Los Angeles Times Mirror who owned New English Library and New American Library as well, they came over intending to close down New English Library because it was a loss making operation. Bob Tanner had just been managing director there and he'd come from wholesale newsagenting and he brought Peter Haining in as the editor. Anthony Cheatham worked there for a time as well and it was such an incredibly low budget operation that year after year it made money. Very few of the books I bought lost money. There's a book by Mervyn Peake's widow *Maeve Gilmore,* I think that probably lost money, but it was still a nice book. We published Mary Whitehouse as well. To have

Mary Whitehouse on the same list as the skinhead books and Harold Robbins, I thought was quite cool.

Home: You reprinted *The Hell-Fire Club* and *The History of Torture* by Daniel P. Mannix.

James: I love Mannix.

Home: Did you ever have any direct contact with him.

James: No. Mannix wrote a book called *Memoirs Of A Sword Swallower*. That was one of my great seminal books when I was about 14 and it was a time when they were bringing out books like Stetson Kennedy *I Rode With The Ku Klux Klan,* these really weird American pulp non-fiction books and *Memoirs Of A Sword Swallower* is a classic of the genre. But I don't know anything about Mannix, or if he is still alive.

Home: You were involved in producing jacket copy. Have you got any particular favourites that you wrote?

James: At the time, because there were only two of us, we would have to do as many as 20 or 25 blurbs a month. You were supposed to spread them out over the month and in fact you had the big production meeting on the last Friday of every month, so normally on the last Thursday of each month, after lunch, Mark Howell and I would do all the blurbs which would be about 25 blurbs between us. We would pass them backwards and forwards to come up with minimalist copy which would say things like "Two men, a town, the gold. They'll come together at rainbow's end." That would be it.

Home: NEL blurbs often took a paragraph out of a novel and stuck it on the back cover.

James: In fact that still goes on. English publishers don't use it all that much but at NEL we'd try to find a nice paragraph to stick at the top of the back cover and that was a third of the blurb done.

Home: I think NEL had more in common with American pulp publishing than a traditional English approach.

James: Mark Howell was an English public schoolboy who came from a background in American mass circulation journalism, and I'd not been involved in paperback publishing before. The traditional paperback end of publishing was simply to publish hardback books in soft covers. You'd go to publishers like Michael Joseph or whoever and they'd send you their hardbacks and you'd buy them and put them out in paperback. That was the traditional way it was done, but that was too expensive for NEL so we originated an enormous amount of material in-house and we had people like Alex R. Stuart, Peter Cave, Chris Priest, Terry Harknett who did the *Edge* western series and they were extremely successful. In the end even the authors made some money out of it, they earned royalties. Even Mary Whitehouse made money. Mary Whitehouse's great skill was she'd give talks, and authors, as you know you're allowed to buy copies at trade, most authors now and again might buy about three copies of one of their books to give to their relatives or whatever, but Mary Whitehouse used to send for about 1,200 copies of her books at trade price and then she'd sell them at her talks and lectures. She did very well out of it.

Home: Was publishing Mary Whitehouse your idea?

James: Yes. My idea originally had been to do a biography of Mary Whitehouse because I thought it would be really interesting to see what the lady was really about. I thought I'd write to her first and ask if she wanted to do an autobiography and when she said no, I'd then go ahead and get a journalist to do a biography. To my amazement Mary Whitehouse agreed to do an autobiography. She was a very enthusiastic, very nice lady. I think a lot of her ideas are incredibly extreme but she is inherently a decent person. I can't mock Mary Whitehouse because she has decent beliefs although she carries them too far. Her ideas about censorship I can't agree with at all, but her basic ideas of protecting young children, you can't really argue against it. As I say she took her ideas too far. But she was good, we got a Foyles literary luncheon for her. The only Foyles literary luncheon NEL ever had in those days. Lord Longford was there, it was good.

Home: To move on to your own writing, how did you get the idea for the first Angels book?

James: I thought I could write, I wanted to try it. I always think the great trick about writing is you can either do it or you can't, like creative writing courses seem to me a waste of time because I genuinely believe you either have the talent or you don't, and you can improve that talent, you can hone it a bit, but if you can't do it, you can't do it. I didn't know whether I could do a novel or not. I'd done short stories and I thought I'd try a novel. The Angels books were about 50,000 words, and so I did the first one, which as I say was bought and was successful and then I did the other three which followed on and they were all successful, they all did well.

Home: So how did you actually set about writing the first one? It was your first novel. What was your actual *modus operandi* for its production?

James: It was triggered by the opening episode at Hither Green station, where there's this long tunnel, because I lived in Hither Green for a time and I always thought it was really creepy, this pedestrian tunnel that ran under the railway. The tunnel was only about five or six feet wide and I always had this nightmare that you'd be walking along late at night and some guy on a motor bike would come thundering down the other way. That was what triggered the opening scene in the book. Everything else came from that. As I say, I'd read Hunter Thompson's book and I'd seen some of the Angels movies. We also wrote two Hell's Angels magazines in-house at NEL. Mark Howell and I wrote those.

Home: I understand you actually made up the interviews with the bikers and Angels.

James: Yes, [laughter], yes. I'm sorry, yes I did, this is true.

Home: No, no I admire that approach.

James: We started off by doing a Johnny Cash magazine. That was the first magazine we ever did in-house because Johnny Cash was booked for a big tour, and so we wrote this magazine and it had lots of personal messages to his fans from Johnny, and we made all that up and in the end he didn't come over but we still sold a lot of magazines, which was really interesting. The Hell's Angels magazines sold extremely well, I mean very, very well.

Home: The Angels magazines are very straight fake reportage, your Angels novels are much more interesting.

James: What I wanted to do was shift the genre a little bit, kind of move the genre sideways from just the straight Hell's Angels narrative to something that was, in a sense, subversive, slightly more political. That was why I set it in the future. A much more reactionary future, which now, I mean, a lot of the things in that did come true in terms of the new Criminal Justice Act which is going to go through. That's the kind of Act that is imagined by making the Hell's Angels actually outlaws. I mean genuine outlaws, not just disliked, but actually illegal. In the same way the Criminal Justice Act will hit at raves and that kind of thing.

Home: So to go back to the first book, you said you got the idea from the opening scene. Before you wrote the book did you know how it was going to end?

James: It wasn't actually going to be a series. I didn't see it being a series of books. I thought there was always a chance. As far as possible, you keep your hero alive. By the time I'd finished the first book and they'd bought it, it then seemed to me there was a strong possibility I could do at least another two. Current events that were happening then find their way into the books. Particularly the police, the power of the police, the increasing power of the police. It was nice to be able to use the Angels. I think the thing about the Hell's Angels is that they are uniquely tribal. There were probably no more than a 1000 serious registered members of the Hell's Angels in America even in their hey-day. In England there was only a tiny handful but what they represented was this incredibly close-knit, Samurai-like closed warrior cult, with their own laws, their own rules, their own ideas of chivalry in the sense of protecting each other. The nearest parallel is probably the masons. A masonic order is a closed order whose members mainly help each other, help themselves and they have their own rules and their own rituals as well. Masonic rituals are actually no more arcane than the rituals of Hell's Angels marriage. I think that's what attracted me, the idea of an outlaw group operating on the very fringes of society.

Home: You allude to the Angry Brigade in the books and say that the anarchists had once been a beacon of hope but now the Angels represented the only hope for freedom.

James: That was never a realistic thought, it was an image. I think tiny fringe groups are a political hope because they're not leaned upon by other large organisations. Groups like the Angry Brigade.

Home: You had no contact with that Notting Hill/Stoke Newington scene?

James: No. Obviously I was aware of it through newspapers and television, but not directly. They were no real influence on the books in that sense at all. One of the things that I enjoyed in the Angels books was putting the small chapters in between which are kind of media parodies of television, film, newspaper interviews.

Home: I thought that was one of the nice things about those novels.

James: Yes. One straight chapter and then the little chapters which I would cut in. I enjoyed doing that. I always enjoy pastiche and parody. You can actually have fake government documents saying really extreme things and you could get away with that and it would work within the structure of the books.

Home: I really like the poem supposedly written by a schoolboy.

James: Funnily enough, last night I was reading through the end of the last book again and I really got quite moist eyed at the end of it and I thought "I like that," because that of course was Brian Jones's death and Jagger reading Shelley at Hyde Park and releasing butterflies. Most of them were dead and they just fell out of the boxes onto the floor, but the idea was nice. That was what triggered that poem in the last Angels book.

Home: I understand you were going to do a fifth Angels book but it was never written.

James: Yes, John Harvey did a couple because by then I'd gone full time. I quit publishing and decided I wanted to be a full time writer and I got contracts to do books for Mayflower and another series for NEL. The NEL series was *Wolf's Head,* which was the Saxon and Norman series which I did with Ken Bulmer, and I did another series for Mayflower called *The Killers* under the name Klaus Netzen, and I did a series for Mayflower about gladiators which was *The Eagles* and that was written by Andrew Quiller, which is a nice pun producing 'aquila', the Latin for eagle.

Home: When I was at school, after I read your books I read the two Harvey novels which were published under the name Thom Ryder. Harvey's prose was much softer than your writing. One of the things I noticed upon re-reading them when I was older were things like the T. S. Eliot references. For example, Thom Ryder has a character called J Arthur Prunefork who'd say things like "that was not what I intended."

James: Yes, John had been a school teacher. I've had a crack at a similar kind of thing, in this series I'm currently doing, this American male action adventure series called *Deathlands.* I'm constantly putting in references and my American editors love it when I put in a little bit of Schiller or a bit of Eliot, bits of Robert Frost and you know, "the woods are silent, dark and deep, I have promises to keep." The editors just love this and I love doing it. I can't resist putting in quotes and pastiches; I put a Mervyn Peake pastiche in the last *Deathlands* book. It's a nice self-indulgent thing to do, but it mustn't ever intrude. You mustn't ever have the reader thinking "Christ, what's going on here, I don't understand this bit, this doesn't make sense." It's got to be part of the book, it's got to work within the structure of the book. So, if people get the joke, that's fine and if they don't it doesn't matter.

Home: To go back to your Angels books, there's the obvious Stones reference with the Angels doing the security at gigs, but are the bands actually based on anyone in particular?

James: I think the glam band was probably based on The Sweet because they were really very heavy glam rock, lots of glitter at the time, but the main band wasn't really based on anybody at all. It was a totally fabricated band. In fact the band has loads of private jokes in it. Isn't the drummer called Chris Rees? Chris Priest. I've got a feeling he is, if I remember rightly. And some of the band tracks have family references and things like that. I think one of the band is Matt David and my two sons are Matthew and David and it's full of stuff like that. Obviously, there are a lot of Dylan references as well.

Home: One of the other things I think is very impressive in your Angels books is the sex. I could imagine you having problems with people at NEL with the levels of sadism in some of the sex. The scene that always stuck in my mind was the young girls who tried to sneak into a pop concert and, after getting caught by the Angels, they are punished by being shaved, covered in glitter and marched naked onto the stage with a whip swishing behind them.

James: Yes, that in a sense spins off from stories like *Plaster Casters* and *Groupie*. Jenny Fabian's book *Groupie* was one of the great books of the time. I read a lot of books about Stones tours and what goes on but I think, in a sense, that's the defence. If people criticise, you say, yeah, but at least I haven't got anybody fucking a dead fish. I mean this is really quite moderate compared to what really goes on.

Home: You had an MP stroking a dog while being beaten by a prostitute.

James: That's utterly realistic.

Home: You never had any criticism over that?

James: No, none at all.

Home: There's quite a lot of cunnilingus in the books, and a lot of homoerotic material. Was that a problem at NEL?

James: Bob Tanner found gay sex quite a problem and we always had to slip that through. The Angels books weren't read by the senior directors. I consciously put in things like the oral sex. People were much more worried about the violence.

Home: What actually gave you the idea for having a chapter of gay Angels in satins who were harder than the straight Angels in leathers?

James: One of the things I always try and do in all my writing is actually to subvert expectations. I thought gay Angels would do that.

Home: You've written a lot of novels since you did the Hells Angel books.

James: I've done a lot, 165 books in 20 years. At times I was doing 14 books a year, westerns, they're only about 50,000 words. Currently with the *Deathlands* series which is this post-nuclear holocaust series set about 90 years after the world has gone, civilisation has vanished, which is really just a futuristic western series, I'm on number 28. These are much longer novels, 125,000 words, so I'm doing six of these a year which is actually more than when I was doing 14 westerns a year. It's all relative. I did twelve *Confessions* books, which was fun to start with but it got very tedious. A lot of westerns, children's books, some with my younger son Matthew that did very well, some horror books, women's fiction under pseudonyms. Altogether, over 150 books under about 20 pseudonyms. Whatever the publishers wanted. Westerns when the publishers wanted westerns, then I moved on when they wanted something else. Films were always a big influence; I'd extrapolate scenes from stuff I'd seen and liked in movies...

There's a lot more on tape after this but it seems like a good place to end because from here I can loop back to my introduction. As I've said, Leon Hunt's *British Low Culture* spurred me into transcribing this interview and he quite correctly observes that film more obviously influenced 'Mick Norman' than 'Richard Allen.' Chapter Five of Hunt's book *'Knuckle Crazy': 'Youthsploitation' Fiction* is a suggestive overview of the relationship between the 'Mick Norman' and 'Richard Allen' books. However, it does me no favours by citing the use I make of 'Richard Allen' in my novels as proof of the greater cultural cachet of the skinhead series. Hunt may be correct about 'Richard Allen's' current standing, but in my early fiction I was making critical use of books James Moffatt wrote under a variety of names, as well as the work of many other authors, most obviously the likes of Peter Cave and 'Mick Norman.' I have read a great many books since I first came across 'Mick Norman' as a twelve-year-old schoolboy but few have had the impact *Angel Challenge* and *Guardian Angels* had on me at that time. I was reading 'Richard Allen,' Peter Cave and Michael Moorcock, but I'd never read anything like 'Mick Norman.' Back in 1974, his books were both thrilling and shocking. This may or may not be nostalgia for a time when there really appeared to be 'no future'.

An abridged version of this interview
appeared in *Entropy 6,* Summer 1998
An extract from the interview is featured on the CD
Hexentexts: A Creation Books Sampler (Codex Books)

ANARCHISM IS STUPID: COMEDY, IDENTITY AND FICTIVE POLITICS

WITH THE COLLAPSE of various state capitalist regimes at the end of the nineteen-eighties, the very marginal position occupied by anarchism within overtly political discourse has been hyped up by the press. For example, in the British Isles, anarchists were given the credit for instigating anti-poll tax riots.[1] While many political theorists appear unwilling to discuss anarchist ideology because it is so clearly mired in the more ludicrous excesses of what can be called 'enlightenment thought', I believe the doctrine demands scrupulous investigation since its totalising responses to social questions mesh with more widespread and equally systematic instrumentalisations of elitism and fear. For some time I have found myself in a favourable position to comment critically upon libertarian culture and politics since fictional interrogations of anarchism have been a feature of my novels and short stories from the mid-eighties onwards.

The deadening effect of anarchist ideologies on critical thinking and debate sometimes appear to be so readily apparent that delineating these eschatological beliefs for anything other than comic effect in fictional form proves tiresome. Writing in the early nineteen-thirties, Max Raphael began his *Proudhon Marx Picasso: Three Essays in Marxist Aesthetics* with the observation:

Any visitor to Paris familiar with Marxist criticism will be surprised to discover to what an extent Proudhon's ideas still influence French 'Communist' politicians, intellectuals, and even artists. But a little reflection will reveal that there is nothing surprising in this. Most artists are of petty-bourgeois origin and their Communism serves to provide them with emotional support, rather than with weapons useful in their practical activities. In point of fact, they are Proudhonians, although – or perhaps because – they have never read Proudhon.[2]

In *Social Radicalism And The Arts, Western Europe: A Cultural History From The French Revolution To 1968,* Donald Drew Egbert notes that since 1793 the term 'anarchist' has often been used as an indiscriminate smear in both the arts and politics.[3] Egbert goes on to trace a number of different anarchist lineages. He asserts there is a socialist or mutualist strain of anarchy that runs through Proudhon, Bakunin and Kropotkin. Somewhat less problematically, Egbert traces a more individualistic English strain of anarchism through figures such as Godwin, Coleridge, Southey and Shelley. I tend to view the latter trend as having exhausted itself in the social snobbery of George Orwell's *1984.* Orwell's novel is archetypically anarchist in its fetishisation of the state as a source of evil and its deification of the bourgeois values embodied in the character of Winston Smith. Nevertheless, Orwell's social pessimism, among other things, has prevented *1984* from being treated as a privileged text within contemporary anarchist discourse.

Among the many novels featuring characters that might be interpreted as anarchists can be listed *Germinal* by Emile Zola, *The Dynamiter* by Robert Louis Stevenson and Fanny Van de Grift Stevenson, *The Secret Agent* and *Under Western Eyes* by Joseph Conrad, *The Princess Casamassina* by Henry James and *Demos* by George Gissing. The relative popularity of novels about anarchists in the forty years prior to 1914 is placed in historical context by Barbara Arnett Melchiori in *Terrorism In The Late Victorian Novel.*[4] The first two chapters document 'terrorist' activity throughout the world as reported by the British press in the last two decades of the nineteenth-century.

Melchiori paints a picture of the escalating use of dynamite for the purposes of social protest. In England political actions of this type appear to have been monopolised by Irish republicans who favoured the symbolic destruction of property. Melchiori suggests that the targets favoured by continental anarchists were quite different: "bombs were thrown into crowded cafés, into restaurants, into opera houses."[5] However, Melchiori contends: "writers did not all succeed in keeping the various historical strands of subversion disentangled."[6]

It seems that this political confusion is not limited to the Victorian period or those who are critical of anarchist doctrines. For example, in *The Bomb* by Frank Harris[7] state support for the arts is advocated by an anarchist character. The blurb on the back cover of a recent reissue of this novel by Feral House is not only politically confused, it is barely literate:

> Called a 'masterpiece' by Aleister Crowley... *The Bomb* focuses on the infamous Haymarket affair, in which a bomb kills police gathered to club and maul labor protesters, and an incredibly unjust trial that later murders five anarchist leaders who had nothing to do with the bomb... *The Bomb* comes from the point of view of the uncaught bomb-thrower, and proves that the kind of terrorism inflicted by the Unabomber and in Oklahoma City emerged as part of political disobedience more than one hundred years ago.

Individuals who had been more actively involved in anarchist politics than Harris were sometimes less sympathetic to the creed when it came to depicting the ideology in novels. For example, Helen and Olivia Rossetti, with their brother Arthur, launched an anarchist publication called *The Torch* in 1891 after being converted to the creed by Prince Peter Kropotkin's *Appeal To The Young*. Later, using the pen name Isabel Meredith, the Rossetti sisters wrote a novel entitled *A Girl Among The Anarchists*.[8] In their book, Helen and Olivia Rossetti treat anarchism as a juvenile diversion and thus an object of humour. Unfortunately, the Rossetti sisters satirise anarchism from bourgeois perspectives that are even more reactionary than the anarchist creed they'd abandoned.

A Girl Amongst The Anarchists is both very different in tone and perhaps less ideologically confused than the future war novels of the pre-1914 period that worked anarchist characters and themes into their plots. A paradigmatic example of this genre is George Griffith's *The Angel Of The Revolution*.[9] Griffith's mix of science fiction, utopian romance and anarchism influenced later writers including H. G. Wells in *The War Of The Worlds* and *The World Set Free*. *The Angel Of The Revolution* features a secret society called the Brotherhood of Freedom who are identified as Nihilists and organised in the manner recommend by the anarchist Mikhail Bakunin and his disciple Sergi Nechaev in the various documents they produced about 'revolutionary' organisation. After the two sides in a world war have inflicted heavy damage on each other, the Nihilists attack them both in fast moving, heavily armoured airships, and go on to establish an international federation under their 'revolutionary' command. Melchiori observes: "there are a number of inconsistencies, suggesting that the author had by no means fully absorbed the doctrine that he was preaching..."[10]

The plot animating G. K. Chesterton's anarchist fantasy *The Man Who Was Thursday*[11] is likely to strike contemporary readers as more believable than *The Angel Of The Revolution*. Chesterton's novel features a Central Anarchist Council who are named after the seven days of the week. As the story unfolds it is revealed that all the members of the Anarchist Council are, in fact, police agents. *The Man Who Was Thursday* has non-fictional counterparts on the outer reaches of conspiracy theory. Esperanze Godot in an article entitled 'Recipes For Nonsurvival: The Anarchist Cookbook', extensively quotes a review from *The Library Journal* to 'prove' that *The Anarchist Cookbook* compiled by William Powell is riddled with errors that endanger anyone using it, then opines:

> The Anarchist Cookbook was originally published in 1971, the
> review by the Library Journal, which exposed these dangerous
> errors, came out shortly thereafter. I wonder why it has gone
> through 28 printings without these errors being corrected. My
> theory is that Mr Powell is not an anarchist, but in reality is
> spreading disinformation to potential enemies of the
> government... Powell's father was a powerful bureaucrat in the
> UN propaganda ministry... My suggestion is that much of
> Powell's disinformation and influence may have come from the
> Trilateral Commission and/or the CIA... [12]

While I was aware of various literary as well as nominally
'factual' representations of anarchists before I began writing
fiction lampooning self-styled incendiaries, it was a series of
chance encounters with the sad skunks producing the Class War
newspaper that provided the necessary motivation for my own
satirical depictions of various anarchist ideologies. In 1985 I had
the misfortune to move to Stoke Newington in North London
and found myself drinking in the same pubs as the Class War
recruitment officer Ian Bone. Back then, Bone's photograph
could be found alongside scare stories in the Sunday People such
as 'Unmasked: The Evil Man Who Preaches Hate to Children'
by Robert Eringer, James Mayer and Trevor Aspinall or 'Inside
The Evil Group Bent On Violence' by Eileen Wise and Robert
Eringer.[13]

To gain an insight into the minds of the Class War editorial
board, one only has to flick through the wearisome Class War: A
Decade of Disorder edited by Ian Bone, Alan Pullen and Tim
Scargill.[14] Surveying this coffee table compendium in the London
Review of Books, Iain Sinclair observed:

> The challenge for the authors of Class War: A Decade Of
> Disorder... is to publish something more meaningful than a

cover version of the rancid tabloids they so obviously model themselves upon... What was being declared here was not so much a class war as a style war... The emblems of defiance – nooses, rubber masks, pirate flags – could have been translated directly from the pages of Richmal Crompton's *William The Lawless,* hinting at safe nursery havens lurking in the undisclosed backgrounds of some of these class warriors... The propensities of the *Class War* leader writers lean more towards the *Beano* or *Dandy* than the tiresome headbutting of French art guerrillas. "Bash the Toffs," "Let your goat into their prize rose garden," "Kidnap their snotty kids." The stratagems are familiar to anyone brought up on the antics of Lord Snooty and his pals, while the topics under discussion rarely deviate from the profoundly conservative programme established by the other tabloids..."[15]

The propaganda of sects like Class War meshed perfectly with the tabloid agenda by enabling the media to ignore issues like police oppression and instead pretend that a handful of 'violent' malcontents were responsible for what was actually broadly based working class resistance to various inequities of the capitalist system. Since Class War's 'activity' consisted chiefly of putting out a thin newspaper every few months and a lot of boasting down the pub, the gap between the group's rhetoric and what it actually did was grist to the mill of anyone interested in producing satirical fiction. I wrote a fifteen thousand word short story about Class War entitled 'Anarchist' in December 1985 and published it the following year in the magazine *Smile*.[16] The piece was reprinted in my short story collection *No Pity*.[17] 'Anarchist' took the early history of Class War, exaggerating and distorting it to comic effect under the guise of a parable about an almost fictional organisation called Class Justice. The Class War mythology was rewritten into a story about leadership rivalry lifted – in places literally – from the pages of a Hell's Angels novel entitled *Chopper* by Peter Cave.[18] In the act of rewriting, the plot of this hack youthsploitation tome was transformed into satire:

> Steve tried to check his thoughts as they took a new and more malicious turn. He wasn't one of the Class Justice sheep, the others looked up to him – but it seemed as though he always had to play the number two to Nick, as if he were a lieutenant and Nick a general... Steve made one final, desperate attempt to push the thought from his head but was unable to stop the nagging doubts – and especially the doubts about Nick. He felt certain Carter was going soft and that Class Justice was being watered down from its original outrageous aims. But, he tried to reassure himself, anarchists don't have leaders and their ideology contained only a single aim – the legalisation of freedom, the crime that contained all other crimes.[19]

Within 'Anarchist' I made extensive use of inversion to parody both anarchism and the types of literature championed in the book pages of English newspapers. The characters in 'Anarchist' were gay because, while Class War endorsed polymorphous perversity, most of those involved in the group were straight and monogamous. Likewise, in my short story I had Class Justice instigate a riot because the tabloid newspapers at the time were running features in which it was absurdly claimed that Class War were capable of doing this. Since I was unlucky enough to regularly encounter the ten or so militant self-publicists who produced the *Class War* newspaper, I was aware that their taste for 'violence' was strictly rhetorical and their 'subversive' activities went no further than spraying the odd piece of graffiti across walls in Hackney.

In terms of literary models, I was drawing on a wide range of teenage reading that included Burroughs, Lautréamont and Alain Robbe-Grillet. There was nothing original in critically appropriating the techniques of pulp fiction for the purposes of parody and burlesque. Where my production differed from earlier exercises of this type, particularly those of the surrealists, was in the choice of material appropriated and the fact that I plagiarised narratives as well as segments of prose. Thus, despite extensive and deliberate use of repetition, my writing might be viewed as a simulation of pulp fiction rather than an example of the representational inscriptions of this form to be found in 'avant-garde' or 'modernist' prose. At the time I wrote 'Anarchist', my meta-fictional interests were focused on an attempt to deconstruct the depictions of sex and violence I found in pornography and pulp fiction with both irony and critical reason:[20]

> Butcher entered the kitchen, unseen, as Dog and Steve vainly attempted to erase the marks of value and exchange inscribed on their bodies by capital and its glistening commodities, as unaware as Butcher that the 'naturalness' of their sexual practice was as carefully constructed by the agents of recuperation as the anarchist ideology they embraced.
>
> Butcher lubricated Steve's arse with margarine, twisted his arms under, up and around Drummond's shoulders, then pumped his seed into the veritable seat of his room-mate's being. The three young anarchists laboured under the illusion they'd re-entered a primitive terrain, an Eden that sexual exhaustion would force them to leave but which could be regained at a later date. They had yet to learn that under capital nothing – least of all "sexual expression" – is natural.
>
> When the mudflats dissolved they were returned to the dirt and grime of their kitchen..."[21]

It is both impossible and undesirable to impose a single monolithic meaning on my fiction; if it communicated a simple and obvious message then it would lack all poetic qualities. Despite the apparent directness of the prose, the text necessarily resists both the reader and the writer. The passage cited above can be read as counterposing proletarian theory (with its use of the terms 'value', 'exchange', 'commodities') to the hollow posturing of anarchism. However, while the critical elements woven into the story draw self-consciously upon left-communist discourse, the simultaneous use of irony results in attempts at reading the text as advocating a clear-cut line of political action being rendered problematic in advance. Some extremely elliptical allusions to the Situationist International do nothing to clarify matters. For example, the term "glistening commodities" does more than simply suggest the sexual organs during and immediately after sex. The pirate English translation of the situationist text *The Society Of The Spectacle* by Guy Debord[22] makes extensive use of the term "shimmering", the phrase "glistening commodities" parodies this. Likewise, the phrase "veritable seat of his room-mate's being" is – among other things – a parodic invocation of a series of documents compiled under the title *The Veritable Split In The International: Public Circular Of The Situationist International* which were first published in 1972.

In case readers hadn't got the point that 'Anarchist' parodied the absurd posturing and rhetorical violence of a non-fictional group of anarcho-bores, the next story to feature Class Justice was entitled 'Class War.' This was first published in *Vague 21*[23] and reprinted in *No Pity*. Once again I used irony and mock praise to ridicule the playground politics of Class War. One of my targets this time was Class War's 1988 'Rock Against The Rich' tour featuring faded pop star Joe Strummer, a public school educated diplomat's son and former lead singer with seventies punk group The Clash. The 'Rock Against The Rich' debacle is partially documented in *Class War: A Decade of Disorder* where Strummer is quoted as saying: "I believe a limit should be put on the property developers. They're driving people out of the city centres. *Someones gotta fight for people* who can't afford their ridiculous prices." [My emphasis.][24]

In theory Class War's rhetoric of violence was directed towards the goal of working class self-defence. Strummer's blather shows that in practice a supposedly intransigent championing of proletarian autonomy was thoughtlessly abandoned in favour of celebrity leadership brought in from outside the class. Since poetics plays a major role in structuring my fiction, the principle target of the mock praise heaped on "Class Justice" in 'Class War' was directed against the aesthetic failings of the group's non-fictional counterpart, rather than their all too obvious (from the standpoint of ultra-leftism) deviations from class positions:

Class Justice had always understood Working Klass Kulture. In the late eighties they'd sponsored a Rap Against The Rich Tour as part of their campaign to bring about the earliest possible demise for bloated yuppie scum. Back then, no-hope Trotskyite organisations were still promoting their cause with the aid of old time punk musicians. Although Steve had dug punk when it was fresh, in his mind it was a dead issue by the end of '77. The Trots had proved just how out of touch they were when their front organisations relied on the services of white rockers. If the left had followed the Class Justice example and used black music as a promotional tool, then the present authoritarian government would never have succeeded in outlawing all forms of communist activism. Back in the eighties those who'd preferred white-boy music to hip-hop failed miserably in the youth recruitment stakes. They had only their reactionary musical tastes to blame for the fact that Europe had long been in the iron grip of the right![25]

It wasn't until I came to write my fourth novel, Blow Job,[26] that I made further use of the almost fictional Class Justice. The initial inspiration for the novel came from hearing there had been a split in Class War and that two separate organisations were using the name. Reporting this under the heading 'Hold The Class War: the real threat is the enemy within', the Independent On Sunday announced: "Class War... has succumbed to that most boring of fringe organisation diseases: The Split."[27] Revealing that Ian Bone and Tim Scargill, two of the three editors of *Class War: A Decade of Disorder* had set up a new Class War organisation, the paper quoted the latter as fulminating against: "middle-class democracy junkies who are only interested in being terribly witty and producing coffee-table reading for the narco-left."

At the time this newspaper article appeared I was working on a novel later published as *Red London*.[28] Bone and Scargill's Class War organisation was a chimera that disappeared after producing a single issue of its street paper. Nevertheless, the summer of 1993 saw me setting to work on *Blow Job*,[29] a novel in which two rival Class Justice groups vie for the allegiance of a handful of militants. My research for the book entailed me attending London Class War meetings, some of which are barely fictionalised in the book:

"Right then," Drummond announced as Tiny handed Dog the implements he needed to minute the meeting. "I'll go through the agenda: 1) minutes of the last meeting; 2) distributing the paper through newsagents; 3) discount for bulk sales; 4) cover for the next issue of the paper; 5) any other business."

"What about getting a crew together so that we can go and ruck the Anglo-Saxon Movement?" Bogroll Bates demanded.

"We'll put that under any other business," Steve was determined that the meeting should run smoothly. "Right, minutes of the last meeting: one, it was agreed that we'd retain the Bronstein Press as our printer because they were prepared to give us ninety days credit on every job, whereas the two firms that gave slightly lower quotes required cash on delivery; two, it was agreed…"

"Hold on," Butcher put in, "I'd like it noted in the minutes that I objected to the decision to use the Bronstein Press and felt that we should use an anarchist printer such as the Bakunin Press. While this might prove slightly more expensive in the short term, it makes more sense to plough money back into our own movement rather than giving hard cash to our political enemies."

"Okay," Drummond assented, "objection noted. Point two, it was agreed that the minimum number of copies of the paper that fully paid-up members of the organisation were expected to sell would be raised from twenty-five to forty per issue."

"What about getting a ruckin' crew together and fuckin' the Nazis?" Bogroll Bates was becoming increasingly exasperated.

"We'll come to that later," Steve responded..."[30]

Class War was nothing but a pose that required the production of a newspaper to enable the group's image to circulate amongst – and compete with – all the other capitalist commodities. Anything that didn't immediately service Class War's media myth was necessarily relegated to "any other business." Although *Blow Job* was written in 1993, contractual complications resulted in it not being published in English until four years later, after my fifth and sixth novels *Slow Death*[31] and *Come Before Christ & Murder Love*.[32] *Blow Job* was first published as a Finnish translation under the title *Oppi Tulee Idästä*.[33] While the four year delay in the English language publication of *Blow Job* could have made the novel appear dated, the fact that anarchist groups tend to operate according to cyclical rather than linear time worked to my advantage. In 1997 the Class War Federation disintegrated and its thirty odd members regrouped into smaller rival organisations, each of which claimed to represent the 'former' Class War. As so often happens with anarchists, a violent image was projected outwards for the benefit of the mass media, while in-fighting absorbed all other energies.

Although I've used fiction as a space in which to explore the ideological ambiguities of anarchism, I would not dispute that the class struggle rhetoric adopted by 'Class War' marks the groups who've used this name recently as relatively sophisticated 'revolutionary' posers. There are other anarchist groups that claim to be 'revolutionary' despite having emerged from the far-right. Neil Palmer uses fiction to interrogate the ideology of one of these groups in his story 'Vegan Reich'.[34] Palmer's tale — which narrates the demise of an eco-fascist group called Dark Green — is an extrapolation from his readings of the *Green Anarchist* newspaper. Whereas I created composite characters by collaging together impressions of actual encounters with members of Class War, Palmer's approach is different in that he draws his inspiration solely from textual sources:

As a Dark Green anarchist, he [Dog] was proud of his grass-roots political convictions. The straight world had fucked the planet up and the Great Mother was about to wreak havoc in return. The seasons were fucked. The trees were dying. Cities were spreading like cancers. Cars were belching out poisonous gas and choking the environment. He'd tried to use unleaded petrol in his van, but the engine was too old to take it, anyhow, his was only one vehicle out of millions used by the straight world! It was only people like him that were making a difference at the moment. The rest of the country deserved to die, squirming in their own vomit, as the cities poisoned themselves to the point of destruction! The Great Mother would protect her children, of course, and he and his kind would be saved! No consumer scum would survive the coming holocaust!

...The Dark Green network was causing a lot of trouble to the authorities. Thanks to their superb line in hyperbole the mass media had credited them with halting the progress of more than a dozen road building schemes up and down the country since the start of the previous year.

Their organisation was well underground, based around a hidden leadership dictating policy which was communicated to regional groups over Britain. They were intent on returning Britain to its true state — an agrarian society organised around self-governing feudal communities. Dark Green was going to give the fat bloated system a gigantic heart-attack! But destroying civilization was not for the faint-hearted..."[35]

The ideology Neil Palmer ascribes to Dark Green is extremely close to that advocated by *Green Anarchist* editors Paul Rogers and Steve Booth. In the mid-nineties these two creeps accounted for at least half the membership of the Green Anarchist 'network' and produced the bulk of its propaganda. Steve Booth's article 'The Irrationalists' illustrates *Green Anarchist's* contempt for ordinary people and the ways in which this meshes with fascist tropes and fantasies of mass murder:

> The Irrationalists commit acts of intense violence against the system, with no obvious motives, no pattern. More important, there is no organisation to claim responsibility, offer explanations, make apologies or demands. Then, with the Tokyo sarin gas attack, Florence Rey and Audry Maupin, the Unabomber, Oklahoma and other such incidents, we entered the age of the Irrationalists.
>
> ONE OFFICE BLOCK, ONE BLUE TRUCK.
>
> The Oklahoma bombers had the right idea. The pity was that they did not blast any more government offices. Even so, they did all they could and now there are at least 200 government automatons that are no longer capable of oppression.
>
> LET A THOUSAND AUM CULTS SARINATE...
>
> The Tokyo sarin cult had the right idea. The pity was that in testing the gas a year prior to the attack, they gave themselves away. They were not secretive enough. They had the technology to produce the gas but the method of delivery was ineffective. One day the groups will be totally secretive and their methods of fumigation will be *completely* effective...
>
> I HAVE A DREAM
>
> One day there will be blue trucks rolling off underground production lines. Missiles will be fired into government

buildings and financial institutions. Politicians will be shot. Mircrolights will spay botulism over every millionaire's ghetto. More beautiful than all this, there will be no organisation claiming 'responsibility', no explanation whatsoever. The whole thing will seem as mysterious as the menacing laughter heard in the Roman baths at Colchester must have been shortly before the Iceni sacked the city...

...The crowd are passive. In their flight from the truth, people submerge themselves in irrelevancy. Aromatherapy, drugs, role-playing games, the lottery, selling Amway. They all have their negative equity mortgages, unemployment, job insecurity, MuckDonalds Happy Meals, *The Sun,* Gulf War Syndrome... In 1992, even after the poll tax and all that, thirteen million brain dead morons voted Conservative. How many will vote for Blair? People pay money for *The Sun.* Millions of them buy lottery tickets. As Mystic Meg once said (echoing Sir Gerald Ratner with his "culture of crap") "The people want trash, so let's give them trash..." All this goes on. Do they act to stop it? Do they bollocks. So in the long run, they get exactly what they deserve, and by *heck* they are going to get it...[36]

While the working class struggles against commodification, *Green Anarchist* applaud fascist bombings and its editors consider money – "people pay money for *The Sun*" – a satisfactory measure of value. Steve Booth and Paul Rogers of *Green Anarchist* are involved in the production and dissemination of hate literature precisely because it furnishes them with ready-made identities while simultaneously bolstering delusions they've cultivated about being persecuted heroes.

Contrary to the intentions of those responsible for the production of self-consciously 'extreme' material, their texts all too readily lend themselves to multiple readings. The limitations of 'extremism' are so flagrantly apparent that earnestly produced propaganda is inevitably destabilised by unintended comic effects. Extremism is always relative. In the case of the anarchist 'organisations' parodied in the fiction I've been discussing, they uncritically accept tabloid newspaper discourse about violence but reverse the moral codes of the mass media. Politics becomes religion, which is another way of saying it becomes kitsch. This is the point of departure for my fiction. However, it is not just in my novels that anything is anything. Starting from what would appear to be very different political perspectives, Alain Besançon in *The Intellectual Origins Of Leninism*[37] and Max Nomad in *Apostles Of Revolution*[38] both see Bolshevism as emerging from the anarchism of Bakunin. Writing as admirers of Lenin but critics of anarchism, Jacques Camatte and Gianni Collu spin a carefully honed variation on this theme in *Origin And Function Of The Party Form*:

> The poverty of the proletariat is its separation from its human nature. This critique supersedes the narrow limits of Proudhon's which was merely a rational impoverishment and thus even a derationalization on the real poverty of man. The Stalinists with their theory of absolute poverty are the real inheritors of Proudhon and E. Sue (cf. Marx's critique in *The Holy Family*).[39]

Fiction is a place in which these and many other issues can be addressed, but it should go without saying that their resolution must remain a matter of social practice.[40] The inability of many journalists and 'critics' to address the fact that working class resistance to capitalism is of far more significance than the farrago of anarchist politics is not really very surprising. These people are, after all, on the whole happy to act as functionaries of the bourgeoisie. Since the function of media discourses structured around the twin fetishes of 'violence' and 'anarchism' is to create the impression that a handful of 'extremists' are responsible for what are in fact manifestations of broadly based class struggle, they must remain a matter of (mis)representation. Regardless of whether anarchism is or is not 'violent', media representations of isolated 'extremists' fomenting 'violence' are intended to mask the fact that since it is under attack, the working class may quite legitimately use force to defend itself and its interests.[41]

Previously unpublished

1. See, for example, the coverage of the Trafalgar Square anti-Poll Tax riot in the *Independent On Sunday* (1 April 1990), in particular the story 'Black flags of anarchy in forefront of fighting' by staff reporters, p. 3.

2. *Proudhon Marx Picasso: Three Essays in Marxist Aesthetics* by Max Raphael, (Lawrence and Wishart, London 1981, translated from German by Inge Marcuse).

3. *Social Radicalism And The Arts, Western Europe: A Cultural History From The French Revolution To 1968* by Donald Drew Egbert, (Duckworth, London 1970, p. 44). In the manner Egbert describes, I have often been smeared as an anarchist. Here, I will restrict myself to one ridiculous example. In 'The War On The Home Front: Comedy and Political Identity in the Work of Stewart Home' included in *Performing Gender and Comedy: Theories, Texts and Contexts* edited by Shannon Hengen (*Studies in Humor & Gender Vol 4*, Gordon & Breach Publishers, Amsterdam 1998, p. 167-177), American academic Kirby Olson manages to slander me as both an anarchist and an anti-feminist.

4. *Terrorism In The Late Victorian Novel* by Barbara Arnett Melchiori, (Croom Helm, Beckenham, Dover and Surrey Hills 1985).

5. *ibid*, p. 8.

6. *ibid*.

7. *The Bomb* by Frank Harris first published by Mitchell Kennerly, (New York 1909), republished by Feral House, (Portland 1996).

8. *A Girl Amongst The Anarchists* by Isabel Meredith first published by Duckworth, (London 1903), republished as a Bison Books edition (University of Nebraska Press, Lincoln and London 1992).

9. This initially appeared as a serial in *Pearson's Weekly* beginning with a synopsis in the issue dated 14 January 1893, then running in weekly instalments from 21 January to 14 October 1893 and amounting to 175, 000 words. Shortly after the final instalment of the story had been published by *Pearson's Weekly*, it was issued in book form by The Tower Publishing Company. For a detailed account of the publishing history of *The Angel Of The Revolution* see 'George Griffith The Warrior of If' by Sam Moskowitz in *The Raid Of 'Le Vengeur' And Other Stories By George Griffith With A Critical Biography By Sam Moskowitz* (Ferret Fantasy, London 1974).

10. *op cit*, p. 132.

11. *The Man Who Was Thursday* by G. K. Chesterton first published 1908, reprint Penguin, (Harmondsworth 1972). It would be futile to attempt to produce an exhaustive list of novels featuring anarchist characters or anarchism as a theme – but to those I've already mentioned one might add the following: *Anarchists In Love* by Colin Spencer (1963), *The Angry Brigade* by Alan Burns (1973), *A Death Out Of Season* by Emanuel Litvinoff (1973), *The Free* by M. Gilliland (1986) and the unbelievably dreadful micro-editions self-published in bound photocopy form by Steve Booth including *City Death* (1993) and *Even Eden* (1994).

12. Included in *Secret And Suppressed: Banned Ideas & Hidden History* edited by Jim Keith, (Feral House, Portland 1993, p. 193–197).

13. 'Unmasked: The Evil Man Who Preaches Hate to Children' by Robert Eringer, James Mayer and Trevor Aspinall, *Sunday People* 27 May 1984. 'Inside The Evil Group Bent On Violence' by Eileen Wise and Robert Eringer, *Sunday People* 10 February 1985. A few more examples of 1980s news coverage of Class War will illustrate how repetitive much of it was. The *Sunday Mirror* of 27 April 1986 carried a front page 'exclusive' headlined 'Royal Wedding Riots Planned' and credited to Nigel Nelson: "Left-wing fanatics are plotting to wreck the Royal wedding of Prince Andrew and Sarah Ferguson... One of our reporters who succeeded in infiltrating the Class War group was told: 'We want to encourage as much trouble and as much hell-raising as possible...' " The *Sunday Mirror* followed this up with another 'exclusive' on 4 May 1986 entitled 'The Enemy Within: Terror plan to "smash the rich scum and their lackeys" '

by Robert Eringer and Nigel Nelson. The latter piece featured the same photograph of Bone and his 'girlfriend' Adrienne as had previously appeared in *Sunday People* on 10 February 1985. The picture was obviously wending its way through the tabloid press alongside reporter Robert Eringer with his Class War 'story'. The picture turned up again in John Merrit's piece 'Exposed – The Fanatics Who Heckled Eastenders Star Lofty' run by the *Daily Mirror* on 17 February 1987.

14. *Class War: A Decade of Disorder* edited by Ian Bone, Alan Pullen and Tim Scargill (Verso, London 1991).

15. Iain Sinclair in *London Review Of Books*, 27 February 1992, p. 5-6.

16. 'Anarchist' by Stewart Home, *Smile 9*, (London 1986).

17. *No Pity* by Stewart Home, (AK Press, Stirling 1993).

18. *Chopper* by Peter Cave, (New English Library, London 1971).

19. *No Pity, op cit*, p. 34.

20. While it is not always useful to make distinctions between fiction and non-fiction, it should go without saying that novelists are rarely 'ideal' readers of their own work in terms of producing 'critical' commentary upon it. It is quite impossible for me to access exactly what 'I' was thinking more than a decade ago. While I always considered anarchists to be utterly ridiculous – and this attitude is evident in my earliest fiction – my reasons for (and ways of) saying this have metamorphosed over the years. Thus, while writing fiction about anarchism has helped me develop and transform my understanding of this form of identity politics, there is a danger that I am projecting the positions to which I currently adhere onto writings that pre-date my arrival at these perspectives.

21. *No Pity, op cit*, p. 43.

22. *The Society Of The Spectacle* by Guy Debord (Black & Red, Detroit 1970).

23. 'Class War' by Stewart Home, *Vague 21*, (London 1989).

24. *Class War: A Decade of Disorder, op cit,* p. 82-3.

25. *No Pity, op cit,* p. 98,

26. *Blow Job* by Stewart Home, (Serpent's Tail, London 1997). This book was the last part of a trilogy in which I was examining the relationship between anarchism and fascism, the two previous novels in this series being *Defiant Pose* (Peter Owen, London 1991) and *Red London* (AK Press, Edinburgh 1994). The link between these books is thematic; there is no overlap in terms of the 'characters' they feature.

27. 'Hold the Class War – the real threat is the enemy within' by Alex Renton, *Independent On Sunday,* 25 April 1993. In fact, as I document in *The Assault On Culture: Utopian currents from Lettrisme to Class War* (Aporia Press & Unpopular Books, London 1988, p. 95-101), the split reported by the *Independent On Sunday* was not the first within Class War. A detailed knowledge of the 1985 Class War split played a crucial role in structuring my short story *Anarchist.*

28. *Red London* by Stewart Home, (AK Press, Edinburgh 1994). This book incorporates passages lifted directly from the sensational Victorian novel *Hartmann The Anarchist: Or The Doom Of The Great City* by E. Douglas Fawcett (Edward Arnold, London 1893).

29. *Blow Job, op cit.*

30. *Blow Job, op cit,* p. 51-2.

31. *Slow Death* by Stewart Home, (High Risk/Serpent's Tail, New York and London 1996).

32, *Come Before Christ & Murder Love* by Stewart Home, (Serpent's Tail, London 1997).

33. *Oppi Tulee Idästä* by Stewart Home, (Like, Helsinki 1995).

34. 'Vegan Reich' by Neil Palmer, included in *Suspect Device: A Reader In Hard-Edged Fiction* edited by Stewart Home, (Serpent's Tail, London 1998).

35. 'Vegan Reich,' *ibid*, p.10–11. Alongside Simon Strong's *A259 Multiplex Bomb "Outrage"* (Codex, Hove 1995), my novel *Pure Mania* (Polygon, Edinburgh 1989) – which is concerned with both rock music and eco-vegan protests – was clearly one of the models for Palmer's story. Palmer's strategy for getting his fiction published is to copy the prose styles of authors who are editing short story anthologies, and then submit the resultant work to them in the anticipation that they will be seduced and flattered by this ruse. Obviously, in the case of 'Vegan Reich' (Palmer's first piece of fiction to be commercially published) this tactic was successful.

36. 'The Irrationalists' by Steve Booth in *Green Anarchist 51,* Spring 1998, p. 11. For critiques of *Green Anarchist* including detailed analysis of their right-wing politics see *The Green Apocalypse* by Luther Blissett and Stewart Home (Unpopular Books, London 1995) and *Anarchist Integralism: Aesthetics, Politics and the Après-Garde* by Luther Blissett (Sabotage Editions, London 1997).

37. *The Intellectual Origins Of Leninism* by Alain Besançon, (Basil Blackwell, Oxford 1981).

38. *Apostles Of Revolution* Max Nomad, (Secker & Warburg, London 1939). To illustrate the wide dissemination and concomitant transformations and distortions of the Bolshevism as Bakuninism thesis as it radiated out beyond the Menshevik circles in which it appears to have originated, I might cite the 'Preface' to a novel entitled *The Flying Submarine* by E. Van Pedroe Savidge (Arthur Stockwell, London n.d.): "It became evident that Bolshevism was a doctrine deeply rooted in the peculiar Russian mentality, and developed by the teachings of Turgeniev, Netchaev, M Bakunin, Herzen and Tkachev into a philosophy, or religion, of destruction." As an example of an ostensibly non-political (but equally eccentric) deformation of the Bolshevism as Bakuninism thesis see *The Messianic Legacy* by Michael Baigent, Richard Leigh and Henry Lincoln (Jonathan Cape, London 1986, p. 131) where drawing on A. P. Mendel's *Michael Bakunin: Roots of Apocalypse,* these authors state: "it can be argued that Lenin's thought owes more to Bakunin than Marx. In its organisation, in its techniques for recruitment, in its means of eliciting loyalty from its adherents, in its Messianic urgency, as Lenin himself acknowledges in his notebooks."

39. *Origin And Function Of The Party Form* by Jacques Camatte and Gianni Collu, (David Brown Publishing, London 1977, p. 5). This is a David Brown translation of a document dating from the early sixties. Through a close reading of Marx's *Grundrisse*, Camatte and Collu went on to break with Bordigist notions of organisation and proceeded to use the pages of the journal *Invariance* as a forum in which to develop the controversial theory that capital had escaped human control and now oppresses a universal human class.

40. It is unfortunately necessary to resist the critical consensus emerging around my work since this could lead to a premature and unproductive closure. Reviewing my novels *Pure Mania* (Polygon, Edinburgh 1989), *Defiant Pose,* and *Red London,* as well as other works such as my short story collection *No Pity,* Iain Sinclair wrote in *The London Review of Books* (23 July 1994): "It's an exercise in futility to complain that Home's novels (which should in any case be read as a single sequence) lack depth, characterisation or complex plots: that is the whole point..." Sinclair's status as a highly regarded and 'trend setting' novelist and critic – alongside the fact that he was the first person to review my fiction favourably in the literary press – resulted in his views being taken up elsewhere. Thus, more recently, Phil Baker concluded a review of *Blow Job* in the *Times Literary Supplement* (6 February 1998) with the observation that: "It would be missing the point to complain about lack of characterization or realism: *Blow Job* is a book in which anything resembling literary value is not just missing but rigorously excluded."

While at the most facile surface levels my books appear to be polarising critical opinion within the British Isles, closer reading indicates an increasing homogenisation. For example Lilian Pizzichin reviewing *Blow Job* in the *Independent On Sunday* (11 January 1998) claimed: "The tone is nasty, the attitude offensive... Home is more interested in the position of the proletariat than following literary trends." While Mike Parker reviewing *Blow Job* in *What's On In Birmingham* (10 January 1998) wrote: "Stewart Home has a certain cult cachet amongst those who claim that his novels pointlessness and artlessness are their very essence. So be it. Let them stick to their inverted snob indulgences and let the rest of us bother with books that at least take you somewhere interesting or challenging." Parker is very much the orthodox critic in his resistance to opening texts up to heterodox readings.

It is difficult to know to what extent the very different critical receptions of 'my' novels in Germany, France and Finland are to be attributed to the process of translation. Interestingly, Oliver Marchart in his *Neoismus: Avantgarde Und Selbsthistorisierung* (Edition Selene, Vienna 1997) treats my fiction as an integral aspect of a more ambitious project encompassing a wide range of aesthetic practices. Marchart's text partially overlaps with – but also productively contradicts – the critical consensus that has grown out of various shallow and not-so-shallow readings of Iain Sinclair's overviews of my work in the *London Review of Books* and *Lights Out For The Territory.* (Granta, London 1997).

The style journalist Steve Beard is one of the few English critics to ignore this growing consensus of opinion in the British Isles. Reviewing *Come Before Christ And Murder Love* in the October 1997 issue of *i-D,* Beard observed: "...The delayed climax which Home obsessively returns to is that moment of ritual human sacrifice which according to Rene Girard's theory of the scapegoat effectively offers a foundational myth for society. The fact that *Come Before Christ* is interrupted by successive acts of mimetic violence suggests that this myth of functional sacrifice is no longer plausible..." Beard was the only reviewer to identify Girard's theory of the sacrifice and the scapegoat as one of the factors structuring this novel. Reviewing *Blow Job* in the April 1998 issue of *i-D,* Beard insolently contradicted dominant critical opinions by concluding: "Who would have guessed it? Home as the saviour of Eng. Lit." While I do not agree with everything either Beard or Sinclair have to say about my fiction, I greatly appreciate their very different forms of theoretical rigor – and the fact that they have developed critical opinions that productively contradict each other.

41. While it is necessary to avoid the anarchist trap of fetishising rioting, the condemnation of rioters by the media and bourgeois political figures is even more ridiculous. That said, those anarchists who fetishise rioting often appear unaware that there is a positive content to revolutionary activity which lies in overcoming alienation and thereby attaining real human community.

INDEX OF NAMES

ABOUT THE AUTHOR

STEWART HOME was born in South London in 1962. His activities and fields of interest have long defied categorisation. In addition to his role as prime propagandist for the Neoist Cultural Conspiracy, Home is a novelist, musician, performance artist and, more recently, an occultist. He is, according to several sources, "an egomaniac on a world historical scale." Home's immense published output includes *Cranked Up Really High, The Assault On Culture, Neoism, Plagiarism & Praxis, Blow Job,* and *Come Before Christ & Murder Love.*

Home continues to live in London where he divides his time between drinking Adnams Suffolk ales and Islay single malts.

ALSO AVAILABLE FROM CODEX

Cranked Up Really High by Stewart Home
ISBN 1 899598 01 4 • 128pp • £5.95 • $9.50
"Shorter, louder, faster" – the definitive treatise on UK and US punk rock.

Satan's Slaves by Richard Allen
New introduction by Stewart Home
ISBN 1 899598 07 3 • 128pp • £6.95 • $10.50
Manson cash-in from leading seventies pulp novelist.

Hexentexts: A Creation Books Sampler
ISBN 1 899598 51 0 • CD • Running time: 62 minutes • £7.95 • $14.95
Features Mick Norman, of seventies Hell's Angels novels, interviewed by Stewart Home.

"i'd rather you lied": Selected Poems 1980-1998 by Billy Childish
ISBN 1 899598 10 3 • 224pp • £9.95 • $17.95

Notebooks Of A Naked Youth by Billy Childish
ISBN 1 899598 08 1 • 224pp • £7.95 • Available in Europe only

Psychoboys by Bertie Marshall
ISBN 1 899598 05 7 • 128pp • £5.95 • $9.50

The Voidoid by Richard Hell
ISBN 1 899598 02 2 • 86pp • £5.95 • $7.95

Flickers Of The Dreamachine edited by Paul Cecil
ISBN • 1 899598 03 0 • 138pp • £7.95 • $11.95

Pussy by Kathy Acker
ISBN 1 899598 52 9 • CD • Running time: 60 minutes • £9.95 • $18.95

To order the above titles send a cheque, postal order or IMO (payable to CODEX, in Sterling, drawn on a British bank) to Codex, PO Box 148, Hove, BN3 3DQ, UK. Postage is free in the UK: add £1 for Europe, £2 for the rest of the world. Send a stamped addressed envelope (UK) or IRC for a full list of available books and CDs.
Email: codex@overground.co.uk